SUN
IN PENANG

Khoo Salma Nasution

*To my mother Linda Ch'ng Cheng Ee and
my sister Su Yin Mustier,
who have been ever so supportive of
my efforts to conserve the historic house
at 120 Armenian Street, and to the memory of
my maternal grandfather Ch'ng Teong Swee.*

PUBLISHED BY
Areca Books
120 Armenian Street, 10200 Penang, Malaysia
Tel (604) 2620123 Fax (604) 2633970
Email arecabooks@gmail.com
Website www.arecabooks.com

© Copyright Khoo Salma Nasution, 2008
All rights reserved

Perpustakaan Negara Malaysia
Cataloguing-in-Publication Data

Khoo, Salma Nasution,1963-
Sun Yat Sen in Penang / Khoo Salma Nasution.
ISBN 978-983-42834-8-3
1. Sun,Yat-Sen, 1866-1925. 2. Chinese--Malaysia--History
3. China--History--Revolution, 1911-1912.
4. Pulau Pinang--History. I. Title
951.08092

CREDITS
Book design by Goh Hun Meng
Layout by Ho Chin Chin
Printed by The Phoenix Press Sdn Bhd, Penang, Malaysia

CONTENTS

Foreword by Lynn Pan	6
Author's Preface	8
Introduction Dr. Sun Yat Sen and the 1911 Chinese Revolution	11
Mobilizing the Nanyang Chinese	17
The Tongmenghui in Penang	31
Sun Yat Sen and the Nanyang Headquarters in Penang	43
Revolution and Martyrdom	71
Dr. Sun's Family in Penang	83
The Legacy of Sun Yat Sen's Supporters in Penang	95
120 Armenian Street *Then & Now*	109
Chronology	120
Bibliography	124
Glossary	126
Index	129

Foreword
by Lynn Pan

A portrait one might call 'The Revolutionary' should, but does not, belong in the imaginary museum of every Chinese. The criteria would be too difficult to set. This becomes apparent the moment you place Mao Zedong next to Sun Yat Sen, two very different revolutionaries. For one thing, the Father of the Republic was extremely well-travelled while the Father of the People's Republic was a stay-at-home. Mao did not make any excursions beyond China's borders until he was 56, and this was only to the Soviet Union. Sun, on the other hand, crossed the ocean from his native Guangdong to Hawai'i when he was still in his teens.

Thereafter you could trace his footsteps all over the world, and he is remembered by museums, memorial halls and exhibitions in a large number of places, from Penang to Kobe. He went to these places to further his revolutionary cause. Indeed, you might say that he was China's first successful international fund-raiser, tapping the wealth and patriotic support of Chinese living overseas.

Far from being greeted with a slammed door, he and his associates found many supporters in Singapore and Malaya. One of these associates, Wang Jingwei, inspired so much admiration that a girl who heard him speak in Penang, Chen Bijun, decided to follow him to Beijing, becoming his accomplice in an attempt on the life of the Manchu Prince Regent there. The two married shortly after the dynasty fell and the Republic of China was inaugurated. Their union is but one of countless examples of the close connections forged between the Chinese in China and the Chinese overseas.

These and many other protagonists in the story of Penang's part in the Chinese revolution are featured in Khoo Salma Nasution's book. The book is doubly interesting for the fact that it is as much about Penang as it is about Sun's revolution. What makes a given dot on the map come alive is the people you find there and why. Fascinatingly and usefully, the book includes a 1920s map of George Town showing the sites associated with Dr Sun and his supporters in Penang. From one of these sites, 120 Armenian Street, Salma has scraped the dust of decades, not only restoring the historic building that stands on it but researching its past to reveal its links to Sun's revolution as well as to her own family.

In this and other ways the book helps the people of Penang to rediscover their own history. I commend it to all those who believe, as I do, that heritage is what provides the places where they live with so much of their character and meaning.

Lynn Pan • Shanghai, August 2007

Author's Preface

It was a fortuitous coincidence that 120 Armenian Street, the premises of the Tongmenghui Nanyang Headquarters in 1910, was acquired by my maternal grandfather in the 1920s.

In 1991, the GTZ-MPPP team spearheading conservation planning in George Town approached me, as editor of *Pulau Pinang* magazine, to research the local history of the Armenian Street-Acheen Street area. During our investigations, my co-researcher Ong Seng Huat alerted me to the historic significance of the house.

The following year, my late grandfather's estate went on sale. Though I never grew up in 120 Armenian Street, the house was of great sentimental value to my mother who had lived there during the Japanese Occupation. In 1993, my family bought the historic property to save it from an unknown fate. I became the custodian.

The house needed urgent repairs. My carpenter and I assembled a motley crew of elderly carpenters, plasterers and painters, and we did our best to restore the house with a small budget and plenty of advice from Malaysian and foreign conservation experts. The work was completed in January 1994.

In 2001, a pictorial exhibition was put up by myself, Lim Gaik Siang and Goh Mai Loon, based on research by Ong Seng Huat. This exhibition was the starting point for the present book.

I am aware that a great number of books and articles have been written on Dr. Sun Yat Sen, covering virtually every aspect of his life. Indeed, I do not claim to present anything new — a great many scholars are far more knowledgeable than I on this subject — but hope that this book will succeed in introducing many locals and visitors to the story of Dr. Sun Yat Sen in Penang.

The text is written in English, and translated into Chinese by Tan Yau Chong. Lim Gaik Siang and Tan Kim Hong have kindly checked both versions for historical accuracy.

Meant for a general audience, this narrative has been somewhat simplified, focusing on only a few central characters. The local context is emphasized, using period photographs and descriptions of Penang. We regret the fact that there are currently no known photographs placing Dr. Sun Yat Sen in Penang; perhaps they will emerge one day.

For the present account, I have relied heavily on Prof. Yen Ching-hwang's seminal work, *The Overseas Chinese and the 1911 Revolution* (1976) as well as his later writings.

I wish to thank friends and fellow researchers Chang Eng Bee, Goh Mai Loon, Kim Phaik Lah, Lim Gaik Siang, Ong Seng Huat, Tan Kim Hong and Teoh Shiaw Kuan, for sharing their knowledge and materials with me. I am grateful to Prof. Yen Ching-hwang, Kwong Wah Yit Poh Berhad, Lynn Pan, Geoffrey Wade, Malcolm Wade, Dr. Cheah Jin Seng and Teresa Kam for the use of illustrations, and to Victor Sun, Percival Sheperdson and Heimun Miksic for their kind assistance.

INTRODUCTION

DR. SUN YAT SEN AND THE 1911 CHINESE REVOLUTION

Sun Wen, known as Dr. Sun Yat Sen to the
West and Sun Zhongshan to the Chinese.
His Japanese alias was Nakayama.

The Young Revolutionary

Sun Yat Sen, aged 17, with a skull cap concealing his Manchu hairstyle.

Sun Yat Sen alias Sun Zhongshan alias Sun Wen was born in 1866 in Chuiheng Village, Xiangshan District, Guangdong Province, a short distance north of Macao.

As a youth, he went to live with his brother Sun Mei in Hawai'i and attended school there. He then studied medicine in the Hong Kong College of Medicine for Chinese (the forerunner of The University of Hong Kong) and worked as a medical doctor in Guangzhou (Canton) and Macao.

Early in his revolutionary career — in 1894 — Dr. Sun formed the Xing Zhong Hui (Revive China Society) in Honolulu. The following year, he staged his first uprising in China, and when that failed, the Qing government put a price on his head.

Dr. Sun then took the first boat out of Hong Kong and found himself in Kobe, Japan. There, he made a break with the past by cutting off his queue, growing a moustache and putting on modern clothes. His new appearance was the first step to becoming an international revolutionary.

Sun Yat Sen as a revolutionary in Japan, Europe and Singapore.

In 1896, while Dr. Sun was in London, he was abducted by the Chinese Legation there, but was rescued with the help of his mentor Dr. James Cantlie. Dr. Sun wrote a book about his experience, entitled *Kidnapped in London*, which launched his reputation as a revolutionary hero to the English-speaking world.

From 1895 until 1912, Dr. Sun spent his years in exile. He became a 'globetrotter with a cause', sailing several times around the world to campaign for the Chinese Revolution.

Globe-Trotting Revolutionary

The second phase of the revolution began when Dr. Sun co-founded the Zhongguo Tongmenghui or Chinese Revolutionary Alliance in Tokyo, Japan, in 1905. It was a loose alliance of several revolutionary groups. Dr. Sun's 'Three People's Principles' (San Min Zhuyi) — Nationalism, People's Power and People's Livelihood — was adopted by the party.

Dr. Sun established a Tongmenghui branch in Singapore in April 1906, and this was elevated to the Southeast Asian bureau or 'Nanyang Headquarters', in 1908.

After Dr. Sun was banned from Japan, he focused more of his efforts on the Overseas Chinese in the

'Wan Qing Yuan', the Tongmenghui headquarters in Singapore (1906-1909). Today it is the Sun Yat Sen Nanyang Memorial Hall, Singapore.

Dr. Sun photographed by Hawai'ian immigration in March 1910, four months before he came to Penang. He entered the United States with false citizenship documents to evade the Chinese Exclusion Laws.

U.S. National Archives and Records

Nanyang, or Southeast Asia. He visited Singapore no less than eight times. From Singapore, the Tongmenghui ventured into British Malaya and the Dutch East Indies, expanding the movement until there were 20 branches and an estimated 3,000 members throughout the region.

Under Dr. Sun's leadership, the Tongmenghui became known as the mainstream of the Chinese Revolution. Altogether ten uprisings in China (and on the Indo-Chinese border), which took place between 1895 and 1911, are associated with him.

After the Xinhai Revolution of 1911, China was declared a republic, and Sun Yat Sen was elected the first Provisional President of the Republic of China.

Although the movement for a Republican China had been successful, China's troubles were far from over. Dr. Sun passed away in Beijing in 1925, amidst power struggles in a divided nation.

Sun Yat Sen and Chinese revolutionaries who fled to the Nanyang after a failed revolt. Photograph taken in Wan Qing Yuan, Singapore.

MOBILIZING THE NANYANG CHINESE

The Nanyang Chinese

As a consequence of its defeat in the Opium Wars, China was forced to open its doors to foreign trade. The opium trade which was so profitable to Western merchants had turned the Chinese into 'a nation of addicts'.

By the turn of the 20th century, Qing dynasty China was in severe decline, suffering from frequent famines, internal rebellions, and incursions by foreign powers.

Decades before that, bad times in China had provoked mass emigration from China to the lands in the Nanyang — literally, 'Southern Seas' — such as the Dutch East Indies, Thailand, French Indo-China, Spanish Philippines and British Malaya. The Overseas Chinese communities made their money from the boom in mining and plantations. They also enjoyed a fair share of the expanding maritime trade between China and the Nanyang as well as across Southeast Asia.

The majority of migrants to Malaya, including Penang, belonged to one of the five speech groups — Fujian (Hokkien), Guangdong (Cantonese), Chaozhou (Teochew), Kejia (Hakka) or Hainan (Hylam) — originating from two provinces in Southern China, namely the Fujian and Guangdong provinces.

Although the Overseas Chinese adapted to their new homes, they maintained strong emotional ties to

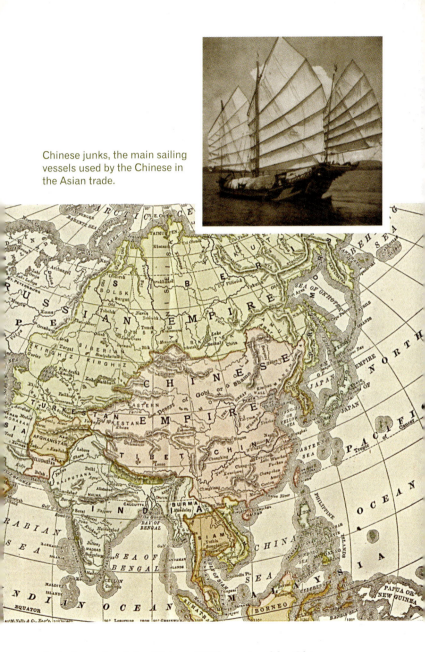

Chinese junks, the main sailing vessels used by the Chinese in the Asian trade.

their homeland in China. With a sizeable Chinese population, Singapore and Malaya became a fertile ground for raising support for causes related to China.

Chinese Society in Penang

Established as a British trading post in 1786, Penang was an important seaport and urban centre in Southeast Asia. It nurtured a cosmopolitan society comprising Malays, Chinese, Indians, Europeans, and other nationalities.

The Chinese in Malaya tended to congregate along dialect lines, but also formed associations according to their district of origin, surname, or clan groupings. Due to the predominance of Fujian people among the early settlers, Minnanhua or 'Hokkien' became the basis of a common dialect among the Penang Chinese.

The most established group of Chinese in Penang was the Straits Chinese, who were recognized as British subjects. Long settled or born in the Straits Settlements before the 20th century, the Straits Chinese had adopted local customs and dress. As merchants, they had the advantage of knowing how to work with the British government as well as European firms. They sent their children to English-medium schools and embraced modernity.

In contrast, the majority of Chinese in Penang and Malaya were Manchu subjects and recent sojourners. Each year, hundreds of young Chinese men came

The main public temple in Penang is the Guang Fu Gong (Kong Hock Keong), or joint temple of the Penang Guangdong and Fujian groups. It is dedicated to the Goddess of Mercy and popularly known as Guan Yin Ting (Kuan Im Teng). The original Chinese Town Hall building can be seen on the right.

through the port of Penang. Some found jobs with their relatives in George Town, where the Chinese worked as shopkeepers, skilled artisans, mechanics or in a variety of other trades. But most were sent out as labourers or 'coolies' to the tin mines of Perak and southern Thailand, or the dreaded tobacco plantations of Deli in Sumatra, to toil under harsh frontier conditions. Penang therefore served as a gateway to these Chinese populations in the hinterland.

A fortunate handful rose from rags to riches to become wealthy merchants.

The Conservative Elite

The Qing Fang Ge (Cheng Hong Kok) in 1897, an elite merchants' club. Some members who have bought Qing honours are showing off their 'mandarin' robes.

Towards the end of the 19th century, the Qing government wooed the wealthy Overseas Chinese by offering official titles and honours in exchange for 'donations' to relief funds. A Consul-General was posted to Singapore from 1877, and a Vice-Consul to Penang from 1893. Through the consuls, the Overseas Chinese could obtain visas to visit their homeland in China.

From 1893 to 1911, the position of Vice-Consul in Penang rotated among five prominent Chinese who were closely allied to each other through marriage or business partnerships. They were not Straits Chinese or British subjects, but Hakkas with ties to the Dutch

The Penang Chinese Chamber of Commerce in 1907, when Wu Shirong sat on the committee.

East Indies. They supported the Qing government's efforts to modernize China by investing in banking, railways and other industrial projects.

Zhang Bishi (alias Thio Tiauw Siat alias Cheong Fatt Tze) was the first Chinese Vice-Consul in Penang. He became Chinese Consul-General in Singapore and eventually economic advisor to the Empress Dowager Cixi.

Photographs on this page reproduced from Twentieth Century Impressions of British Malaya, *1908. Courtesy of Cornell University Library, Southeast Asia Visions.*

Championing China

Hugh Lo

In Singapore and Malaya, a fierce debate raged among three groups who claimed to champion the political and economic salvation of China — the conservative pro-Qing elite, the reformists and the revolutionaries.

The Qing government coopted the wealthiest Chinese and wooed them for funds and expertise to modernize China.

The reformists advocated constitutional reforms and the introduction of a parliamentary system.

The revolutionaries called for the complete overthrow of the Qing dynasty and Manchu regime, in order to pave the way for a modern Chinese nation.

All three groups targeted the overseas Chinese as a source of support and funds. Through their competing activities, the overseas Chinese started to become politicized and imbued with the spirit of Chinese nationalism.

A show of Chinese patriotism — shops in the mining town of Ipoh, Perak, displaying the yellow dragon flags of Qing dynasty China, pre-1911.   *Postcard courtesy of Cheah Jin Seng.*

When Sun Yat Sen shifted his focus to Singapore and Malaya, he found that the reformists had already established their influence here. Sun's strategy was to engage in a polemical war against the reformists through public speeches and newspapers.

In China, foreign penetration advanced while the Qing government's attempt to implement constitutional reforms was slow and unconvincing. Finally, the death of Emperor Guangxu in 1908, followed closely by the death of the Empress Dowager Cixi, turned the tide of popular opinion in favour of the republican revolutionaries.

Revolutionaries Amongst Us

Among the Tongmenghui leaders who worked closely with Sun Yat Sen in Singapore and Malaya were Hu Hanmin, Huang Xing and Wang Jingwei. All three had been students in Japan and were to become important players in Chinese nationalist politics.

The reputations of Dr. Sun, Hu Hanmin and Wang Jingwei were augmented by their writings in *The Minpao Magazine*, a revolutionary paper which was also read in the Nanyang.

From 1907 onward, many Chinese in Singapore and Malaya had the opportunity to meet and listen to Dr. Sun and his close associates; quite a few could even claim to be their personal friends.

Hu Hanmin (1879—1936)
He was the Tongmenghui's leading intellectual, editor and writer for *The Minpao Magazine* and leader of Dr. Sun's core Cantonese faction. He became the first republican Governor of Guangdong.

Huang Xing (1874—1916)
Co-founder of the Tongmenghui in Japan, he represented the Hunan-Hubei faction of the revolutionaries. He led several insurrections between 1905 and 1911. He was made War Minister and chief-of-staff of the armed forces of the provisional government in 1912.

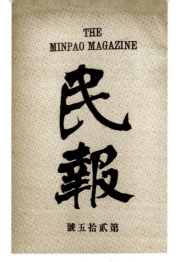

The Minpao Magazine, or **Min Bao** (literally 'People's Journal'), the Tongmenghui mouthpiece, founded in Tokyo in 1905. Revolutionary newspapers were run by the party's leading intellectuals to fight a polemical war against the Qing government and the reformists.

Wang Jingwei (1883—1944) A graduate in constitutional law and political science and a brilliant polemicist for *Min Bao*. He spent much time campaigning in towns from Singapore to Rangoon. He married Chen Bijun from Penang. In 1910, he tried to assassinate the Manchu Prince Regent and was imprisoned until the Wuchang Uprising. In 1924, Wang was made a member of the Guomindang Central Executive Committee. After the Second World War, Wang and his wife were vilified as traitors to China for collaborating with the Japanese to set up the war administration in Nanjing.

Chen Bijun (1891—1959) A Penang-born woman pioneer, the daughter of a conservative Cantonese gold merchant father and a pro-revolutionary mother. The romance between Wang and Chen was the talk of revolutionary circles. Chen and her two mothers bankrolled Wang's assassination attempt and the subsequent campaign to rescue him from a harsh prison sentence.

SUN YAT SEN IN PENANG

Call To Save China

Political cartoon showing the Manchu government trying to stop China being carved up by Britain, Germany, Russia, France and Japan.

Sun Yat Sen spent decades cultivating his wide contacts and intelligence network among the maritime Chinese around the world. He knew how to address each group and play on their sympathies. Speaking to the Overseas Chinese at the Ping Zhang Gong Guan (latterly called the Penang Chinese Town Hall) in 1907, Dr. Sun appealed:

Ladies and gentleman, China is now in a very dangerous position. It can be partitioned by the foreign powers at any time. But the Manchus are fearful and nervous, and are under the foreigners' control. They are willing to be the servants of the big powers, such as Britain, France, the United States, Russia and Japan. But the Manchus oppress us ruthlessly and enslave us. Would we, the Han Chinese, not become the slaves of the slaves? ... Our Principle of Nationalism, one of the Three People's Principles, is to seek equality with the foreigners, and not to be their slaves.

Yen Ching-hwang, The Overseas Chinese and the 1911 Revolution, *p.332*.

Resist the Qing, Restore the Ming

The Overseas Chinese were urged to be patriotic to China, but at the same time, to revolt against the Chinese government. The revolutionaries reasoned that the Qing dynasty represented foreign Manchu domination over the Han Chinese and so should be overthrown.

The Overseas Chinese could identify with this call, for in many cases their ancestors belonged to secret brotherhoods which had sworn to 'Resist the Qing and restore the Ming'.

Speaking at the San Shan Club in Penang, Wang Jingwei played up the anti-Manchu sentiment among the Fujian audience:

The main reason your ancestors migrated here was to escape persecution and enslavement by the Manchus after Zheng Chenggong's regime in Taiwan was conquered. They continued to fight to maintain their identity as the subjects of the great Ming Dynasty.

As your ancestors were so patriotic, how could you forget their enmity towards the Manchus? The aim of our revolutionary movement is to avenge the persecution of our ancestors and to recover our lost nation.

Our Fujian compatriots must respond fervently to the revolutionary appeal, and help the revolution to succeed. By so doing, you will console the spirit of your ancestors in heaven.

Yen Ching-hwang, The Overseas Chinese and the 1911 Revolution, *p.339.*

THE TONGMENGHUI IN PENANG

Wu Shirong (Goh Say Eng), Dr. Sun's loyal supporter and Penang's leading revolutionary. From 1910, he was the mainstay of the Chinese revolutionary movement in Malaya.

Reproduced from The Overseas Chinese and the 1911 Revolution.

The bustling Weld Quay waterfront, circa 1920. Penang was an important port on the international steamship route.

A map of British Malaya (now West Malaysia) showing the steamship lines and submarine telegraph connections between Penang and Singapore in 1897. Penang, Melaka and Singapore were part of the former British Straits Settlements, up till Malaysian independence in 1957.

Courtesy of Frances W. Pritchett, Columbia University.

SUN YAT SEN IN PENANG

32

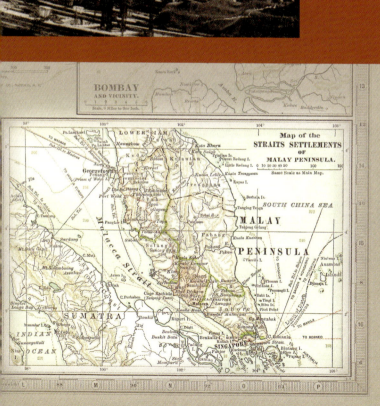

The First Public Talks in Penang

When Dr. Sun Yat Sen first came to Penang in 1906, he stayed at the Xiao Lan Ting club. Dr. Sun was supposed to meet a Penang tycoon, through an introduction from a Mr. Khoo of Kuala Lumpur, but this tycoon refused to meet him. Fortunately, Dr. Sun met Wu Shirong, Huang Jinqing, and a few others who were enthusiastic to hear about affairs in China. As members of the club, Wu Shirong and Huang Jinqing arranged a farewell dinner for Dr. Sun and invited many of their friends. Dr. Sun's talk stunned the conservative audience, who simply walked off.

In 1907, Dr. Sun, Huang Xing, Hu Hanmin and Wang Jingwei visited Penang. While speaking at the Penang Chinese Town Hall, they were heckled and denounced by the reformists. Some reformists pulled out of the Town Hall, pressuring the committee to

tighten their rules to prevent the Town Hall from being used for anti-Manchu propaganda. The new rules would require speeches to be vetted by a committee.

Initially the revolutionaries met with a cold reception among the conservative business community. 'Everyone looked at the revolutionaries as though they were snakes and scorpions.' They likened the revolutionaries to those who had 'no father, no emperor'. After a talk by Wang Jingwei, a businessman even challenged sarcastically, 'If the revolution succeeds, I will jump into the sea and die!'

But the revolutionaries persevered in their mission. In Dr. Sun's view, the main role of the Overseas Chinese in the revolution was to bankroll it. With regard to a certain merchant in Kuala Lumpur, Dr. Sun advised his supporter :

First move him by the importance of our cause. If that is not successful, then move him with the rewards that will come out of this investment. I suppose that you have used both these arguments without effect. But there is one more argument, the argument of friendship and sentiment. You all know him very well and are very close friends. Then you must use your friendship to persuade him. ... If he does give us this 100,000 dollars, then we promise him the monopoly rights to all the mineral resources of the province of Yunnan for ten years.

Wang Gungwu, Community and Nation, p. 136.

An early 1880s view of the Ping Zhang Gong Guan, the precursor of the Penang Chinese Town Hall, at Pitt Street. It was controlled by pro-Qing conservatives and reformists. Sun Yat Sen gave a speech here in 1907.

The Penang Philomatic Union

The revolutionaries initially tried to win over the wealthy tycoons, merchants, tin-miners and plantation owners, but had limited success. Later, they broadened their appeal to smaller shopkeepers, petty traders, teachers, clerks, shop assistants, tin-mine and plantation workers, gardeners, hawkers and even rickshaw pullers.

In 1908, Wu Shirong called a meeting of the Tongmenghui at his villa, Rui Fu Yuan (Swee Hock Hui) on Ayer Itam Road. He said that Dr. Sun had instructed them to set up a newspaper and also a reading club. While they did not have the funds for a printing press, they decided to go ahead and form the reading club, naming it Bincheng Yueshu Baoshe.

The English name – Penang Philomatic Union – was suggested by Lin Zisheng and ratified by Dr. Sun. Wang Jingwei, who was on his way from Singapore to Burma, was persuaded to stay for a few days to draft the constitution. Before the year was out, a notice was sent out to announce a public meeting.

On the 13th of this 11th lunar month (6 December 1908), on Sunday noon at the Chinese Town Hall, we plan to start up the Penang Philomatic Union and have sought approval from the British Protector of Chinese. We hope those who are interested in common objectives will come and give your opinion and support.

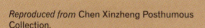

本月十三日禮拜上午十二點在平章會館集議開辦椊城閱書報社。業經請准華民政務司屆期務望熱心公益之同志玉臨賜教有厚望焉謹此奉覽

發起人吳世榮黃金慶陳新政丘明昶楊彩霞熊玉珊陳夢齡丘開端丘兆熊饒純齋李慕參林紫盛林挺生裕生薛南黃奕坤李公劍鄧兆侶沈瑞意古偉堂林建春岑憲臻林和財張偉楊如金　贊成人梁從雲林貽博宋煌發饒集蓉陳瑞東張顯辰李鳳苞曾集棠陳文波

Reproduced from Chen Xinzheng Posthumous Collection.

Notice of the Penang Philomatic Union inaugural meeting

Founding members:
Wu Shirong, Huang Jinqing, Chen Xinzheng, Qiu Mingchang, Yang Caixia, Xiong Yushan, Chen Mengling, Qiu Kaiduan, Qiu Zhaopi, Rao Chunzhai, Li Mushen, Lin Zisheng, Lin Tingsheng, Yu Shengchun, Xue Nan, Huang Yikun, Li Gongjian, Deng Zhaolu, Shen Ruiyi, Gu Weitang, Lin Jianchun, Cen Xianzhen, Lin Hecai, Zhang Wei, Yang Rujin.

Supporting members:
Liang Congyun, Lin Yibo, Song Xuanfa, Rao Jirong, Chen Ruidong, Zhang Xianchen, Li Fengbao, Zeng Jitang, Chen Wenbo.

Wu Shirong was elected founding president, and many of the Philomatic Union members were also Tongmenghui members. The society was duly registered with the Chinese Protectorate.

More Than A Reading Club

The Penang Philomatic Union was inaugurated at the end of January, 1909. Its initial address was 94 Dato' Kramat Road — premises either belonging to or leased by Huang Jinqing. The Penang Philomatic Union grew from strength to strength and became the most successful reading club in Malaya and Singapore. Its public talks and cultural activities attracted large audiences.

'Blue Sky, White Sun'. The Tongmenghui flag was flown at the Penang Philomatic Union premises.

The first premises of the Penang Philomatic Union, a bungalow at 94 Dato' Kramat Road.

Apart from the Penang Philomatic Union, two other reading clubs were started in Penang — Gong Yi in Balik Pulau headed by Xu Ruilin and Hua Qiao in Bukit Mertajam headed by Lin Shi'an. Huang Jinqing's Wei Xin reading club was another front for the revolutionaries.

Autographed portrait of Dr. Sun Yat Sen presented to Xu Ruilin (Chee Swee Ling), founder of the Balik Pulau reading club in Penang.

The Tongmenghui, an underground organization in British Malaya, conducted its activities under the cover of reading clubs. Over 50 reading clubs were established in Malaya and Singapore. Besides offering a wide range of books, magazines and newspapers, these propaganda centres also circulated revolutionary literature and organized talks by local and visiting revolutionaries.

The reading clubs served as recruiting ground for new Tongmenghui members. Anyone wishing to join had to take an oath before one of the central party members. He or she also had to sign a form which would be sent to the Tongmenghui headquarters in Tokyo, which would issue the new membership number.

'Revolutionaries recognize each other by using a password. One of them will ask "What matter? What things? What people?" The correct reply is "Zhong Hua [China]." Then they shake hands, using four fingers, instead of five.'

Penang Stalwarts

The second premises of the Penang Philomatic Union at 120 Armenian Street.

In May 1909, the Penang Philomatic Union moved to 120 Armenian Street, which was more conveniently located. These premises witnessed the most significant chapter of the Philomatic Union's history.

In April 1910, Wang Jingwei was arrested for attempting to assassinate the Manchu Prince Regent. The news so deeply affected his Penang comrades that they desperately tried to raise funds towards securing a mitigation of his prison sentence in Beijing.

Time and again, members of the Penang Tongmenghui demonstrated great commitment and self-sacrifice. Even when Sun Yat Sen's leadership was challenged elsewhere, the Penang Tongmenghui members stood by him. Wealthy leaders like Wu Shirong and Huang Jinqing devoted all their resources and personal fortunes to the revolutionary cause.

Wu Shirong alias Goh Say Eng was born in Penang in 1875. A wealthy merchant, he was the founding chairman of the Penang Tongmenghui and the Penang Philomatic Union. He was a pillar of the revolutionary movement in Malaya. In 1912, he represented the Nanyang Chinese at the Tongmenghui national convention in Shanghai.

As a young man, Wu Shirong inherited a large fortune and the family business Chop Swee Hock, a Chinese factory making flour, rice noodles and safety matches. He spent his own wealth and his wife's inheritance on the Chinese Revolution.

During the Japanese Occupation, he was discovered by a Japanese officer — his son by a Japanese mistress — who had him spared from ill treatment in the final months of his life. He died a pauper in 1941.

Huang Jinqing alias Ng Kim Kheng was a miner from Siam who later settled down in Penang. He was founding vice-chairman of the Penang Tongmenghui and the Penang Philomatic Union.

Chen Xinzheng alias Tan Sin Cheng was a founding member of the Tongmenghui. He later started two prominent Chinese schools in Penang, the Chung Ling School and the Fukien Girls' School.

Qiu Mingchang alias Khoo Beng Cheang **Xiong Yushan** **Yang Hanxiang**

DR. SUN AND THE NANYANG HEADQUARTERS IN PENANG

Sun Yat Sen in the winter of 1910.

Reproduced from A Photo Album of Sun Yat-sen in Macau.

Penang was ideally suited to serve as a communication centre for organizing a remote revolution. The revolutionaries used British banks to remit funds to Hong Kong and telegraph offices to cable their coded messages. Sea travel and railway travel were integrated, so that a passenger arriving by ship in Penang could immediately take a train to the west coast Malayan states.

Penang, circa 1910. **Above,** modern banks on Beach Street. **Right,** the F.M.S. Railway building, Penang.

Photographs courtesy of Geoffrey Wade

Transferring to Penang

After a successful year-long campaign in America, Dr. Sun sailed east to Japan but could not stay as the ban upon him was still in effect. He arrived in Singapore on 11 July 1910.

In Singapore, the anti-Sun faction of the Tongmenhui had stirred up misgivings over his leadership. Dr. Sun realized that he would receive little support there. Therefore, he consulted his close associates in North Malaya about relocating his headquarters to Penang. This plan met with great enthusiasm among the Penang Tongmenghui.

On 19 July, Dr. Sun sailed in a German steamship to Penang and was met upon arrival by Wu Shirong, Huang Jinqing and others. He initially stayed at 94 Dato' Kramat Road for several days before moving to a rented house at 400 Dato' Kramat Road. Dr. Sun moved again to a larger house at 404 Dato' Kramat Road some weeks later, when his family came to join him in Penang.

Dr. Sun originally intended to return to Singapore after a week or two, but changed his mind and stayed on in Penang. He instructed Zhou Hua, the secretary of the Nanyang Headquarters, to move up from Singapore to Penang and to bring along all the party papers. The transfer of the Nanyang Headquarters was effected by August 1910.

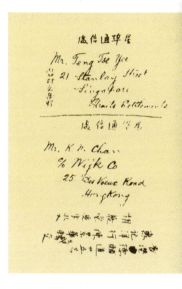

Letter to Wu Zhihui in Hong Kong, written by Sun Yat Sen on board the Norddeutscher Lloyd, Bremen, *Dampfer Roon*, on the voyage from Singapore to Penang, 20 July 1910. Dr. Sun wrote about meeting up with his comrades on Penang island, and the urgency of rescuing Wang Jingwei.

Reproduced from Calligraphy Treasures of Zhongshan, Volume 6.

Reorganizing the Tongmenghui

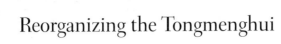

Sun Yat Sen appointed Penang Tongmenghui leaders Wu Shirong and Huang Jinqing as President and Vice-President, respectively, of the Nanyang Headquarters. Chen Xinzheng, Xiong Yushan, Qiu Mingchang and Yang Hanxiang were also given key positions. A standing committee of seven sections was created, consisting of executive, finance, secretariat, external affairs, education, investigation, and social functions. With the transfer, Penang superseded Singapore as the centre of the revolutionary movement.

Revolutionary fervour in Singapore and Malaya were generally on the ebb. In order to give the Tongmenghui a new impetus, Dr. Sun set about reorganizing the party, weeding out dissenters and firming up the machinery. He organized the party rank and file along military lines, with a hierarchy of cell groups and a clear chain of command.

Dr. Sun had earlier introduced a new party name 'Zhonghua Geming Dang' (Chinese Revolutionary Party), as the Tongmenghui had been blacklisted by the British and French colonial governments. Now Dr. Sun demanded that all members, old and new, swear themselves in under the new party name and take an oath of loyalty to him. The Tongmenghui branches, however, would still be referred to as such.

Dr. Sun continued to write letters to his supporters around the world, motivating them to raise funds for

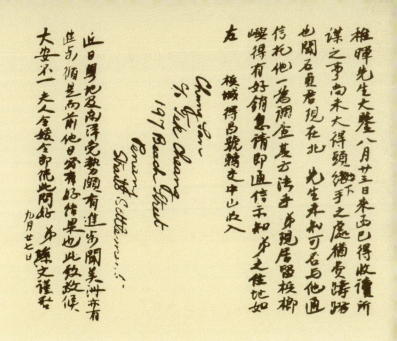

Letter to Mr. Wu Zhihui, written by Sun Yat Sen in Penang, September 27, 1910.
Reproduced from Calligraphy Treasures of Zhongshan, Volume 6.

the next uprising. Tongmenghui representatives from all over Malaya came to seek an audience with him at his house in Dato' Kramat Road. Dr. Sun also dropped in frequently at 120 Armenian Street to guide the workings of the Nanyang Headquarters.

Henceforth, Dr. Sun steered the revolutionary movement from his stronghold in Penang. He was determined to go his own way, bypassing the Tokyo headquarters and the anti-Sun factions in the Tongmenghui. For this reason, the Southeast Asian bureau in Penang might even justifiably be called Dr. Sun Yat Sen's Nanyang Headquarters.

The seal of Zhonghua Geming Dang, Penang branch.

The Penang Conference at 404 Dato' Kramat Road

From Penang, Dr. Sun masterminded an uprising to capture Guangzhou (Canton city) in southern China as the revolutionary capital. Dr. Sun called a meeting — subsequently known in history books as 'The Penang Conference' (*Bineng Huiyi*) — to plan the Second Guangzhou Uprising. The meeting took place on Sunday, 13 November, 1910 (12th day, 10th lunar month) at his house at 404 Dato' Kramat Road. The participants were:

> Sun Yat Sen, chairing the conference
> Huang Xing
> Hu Hanmin
> Zhao Boxian (Zhao Sheng)
> Sun Mei, Sun Yat Sen's elder brother
> Wu Shirong, Nanyang Headquarters
> Huang Jinqing, Nanyang Headquarters
> Xiong Yushan, Penang
> Lin Shi'an, Penang
> Deng Zeru, Kuala Pilah branch
> Li Xiaozhang, Ipoh branch
> Li Yixia, Pontianak branch

The Tongmenghui headquarters in Tokyo was not told of this meeting, and the party leaders who opposed or doubted him were not invited. Dr. Sun only called his most trusted followers and those representatives of the Tongmenghui branches in Southeast Asia who were loyal to him.

Dr. Sun convinced his comrades that his strategy had a good chance of success. The Qing authorities would

Dr. Sun's office and family home at 404 Dato' Kramat Road. It was a double-storey bungalow set in a walled compound.

let their guard down as they would not be expecting another uprising so soon. Though the revolutionaries had experienced failure in the past, this time the uprising would be meticulously planned and backed by adequate preparations.

What our comrades are hesitating over is the lack of funds and arms. But most of you fail to realize that after a series of uprisings, and due to the publicity efforts of our comrades in overseas cities and towns, the spirit of revolution has permeated the Nanyang archipelago.

The Penang Conference confirmed Guangzhou as the target of the planned revolt. Five hundred 'dare-to-die' revolutionaries would be recruited as the vanguard. The battle would be won by the New Army troops who had defected to the side of the revolutionaries some months earlier.

Fundraising targets were set — $50,000 from British Malaya, $50,000 from the Dutch East Indies, $30,000 from Thailand and $30,000 from French Indo-China, with a total target of $130,000 or a minimum of $100,000 (Straits dollars). The money would be collected in the name of an 'Education Fund' to avoid detection by the colonial governments.

Emergency Meeting at 120 Armenian Street

The military leader Zhao Sheng needed to return quickly to Hong Kong with funds to make preparations for the uprising. Due to the urgency of the matter, a second meeting was convened the very next day, that is, on Monday, 14 November 1910 (or 15 November, according to some historians). The fundraising campaign for the Second Guangzhou Uprising was launched at this meeting, held at the Nanyang Headquarters.

Sun Yat Sen chaired the Emergency Meeting and gave a moving speech. In appealing to his supporters for funds, Dr. Sun used the classic Chinese analogy of 'The Last Battle', that is, 'breaking the plates and sinking the boats'. He urged his supporters to give their all. With this battle, it was a 'make or break' for the Tongmenghui — there would be no turning back. The speech was transcribed by Nanyang Headquarters committee member Yang Hanxiang, who remarked:

> *Tears streamed down the President's cheeks while he spoke in a voice full of indignation, and all the comrades were deeply moved. Although economic conditions were quite difficult at that time, the comrades, encouraging each other, gave donations generously. Due to the absolute sincerity of the President, a total of over 8,000 dollars was raised.*

The Penang contribution was later topped up to $11,500 (Straits dollars); this made up about a quarter of the total amount contributed by the Chinese in Singapore and Malaya. The significance of the Penang supporters' contribution is even greater if we consider that they were already carrying the burden of the Nanyang Headquarters and Dr. Sun's household expenses.

Colonel Zhao Sheng alias Zhao Boxian,
the top military strategist and leader of the New Army regiment which had earlier mutinied and defected to the revolutionary cause. After the Emergency Meeting, he immediately returned to Hong Kong with the funds required to keep the troops together. After the failure of the Second Guangzhou Uprising, for which he blamed himself, the heartbroken Zhao succumbed to illness and died soon afterwards.

The quotations on pages 51-55 are taken from Yang Hanxiang, "The speeches of the President in Penang pertaining to the Planning of the 1911 Canton Uprising."

Sacrifice for the Revolution

Every time I meet with you, there is no other reason except to persuade you to donate [for the revolutionary cause]. From the start all of you have been enthusiastic about the party's affairs, and have spared no effort in helping the party. You might think that the party's efforts are in vain; after so many unsuccessful attempts, I myself feel very uneasy and regretful before all of you.

However, at this time — as our country is surrounded by great powers and yet the Manchu government is so fatuous and incompetent — if we don't not act soon, our country will perish.

The situation is so precarious that we do not know at dawn what may happen by dusk. Moreover, despite its unfortunate failure, the New Army's insurrection in Guangzhou during early spring has sowed the seeds of revolution among the military forces across China. Among these military forces, there are many who clearly know the trend of the world and agree with our party's doctrines. On the surface they still belong to the Manchu government, but in actuality they are already our comrades; once the time is ripe, they will change sides and fight for our party. Therefore, we believe this is the best opportunity for us to restore the sovereignty of our country, and we will spare no effort to achieve this goal.

Sun Yat Sen's speech at the Emergency Meeting of the Southeast Asia Tongmenghui at the Nanyang Headquarters, 120 Armenian Street.

As I have said just now, every time when I meet with you, I always ask for your donations. I do not want to do this, actually; but with the burden of responsibility on my shoulders, who else can I ask help from, if not from you, my sympathetic comrades? Therefore, though unwilling, I have no other choice but to ask you for donations.

You can help shoulder the responsibility of saving our country by donating your money, while our comrades in our country are sacrificing their lives.

In short, donating money is a duty that all of you cannot shirk. Please understand this situation and make donations enthusiastically so that the last attempt of ours will turn out successfully.

If heaven does not bless the Han people and the forthcoming uprising fails, I will not trouble you again by asking you for another round of donation. Even if I survive, I will be too embarrassed to face you again. It will then depend on all of you to continue shouldering together the burden of the unfinished revolution. In short, success or failure, and however difficult the situation may be, this time the party will go all out for the 'Last Battle'. Here I conclude my speech.

Controversy in the Press

Just before the Penang Conference, Dr. Sun's activities in Penang became the subject of public controversy. He was invited by some prominent members, including Zhuang Qingjian (Choong Cheng Kean) to speak at the Qing Fang Ge (Cheng Hong Kok) or Chinese Merchants' Club. The speech was reported in the *Penang Sin Poe*, a conservative Chinese paper. The European editor of the *Straits Echo* then condemned Sun Yat Sen and the revolutionary movement in a most sarcastic tone:

The only fault we have to find with Dr Sun Yat Sen as a revolutionary is that he doesn't revolute... For with Dr. Sun Yat Sen it seems money, money, money all the time, and never anything to show for the stream of gold that has flowed his way...

A supporter of Dr. Sun wrote in to the *Pinang Gazette* to criticize this biased reporting, but the *Straits Echo's* editor had the last say.

Years later, Yan Hanxiang recounted that even though he and Wu Shirong could not read English, they bought copies of the *Straits Echo* and the *Pinang Gazette* and brought them to Dr. Sun at his Dato' Kramat residence. Sensing their dismay, Dr. Sun just smiled and said, 'I am used to it. ... We are staying in a foreign land and can easily be faulted for whatever we do. Since we don't have an English newspaper, how can we fight a polemical war against them?'

Right, the Qing Fang Ge on Macalister Road.
Middle, the masthead of *Penang Sin Poe*.
Bottom, *Straits Echo*, 2 November 1910.

Revolutionary Press

In Penang, the Chinese newspaper *Penang Sin Poe* was often used by the conservative elite to denounce the revolutionary movement. In response, the Penang Tongmenghui felt that it was necessary to establish their own newspaper to get the revolutionary message across.

Zhuang Yin'an and the 'Burma Chinese Times' or *Yan Kon Kwang Hwa Pao*

Reproduced from The Overseas Chinese and the 1911 Revolution.

The Tongmenhui's revolutionary newspapers such as *The Minpao Magazine* in Tokyo and *Chong Shing Yit Pao* in Singapore crusaded against the Manchu regime and the reformists. In 1910, the Singapore paper *Chong Shing Yit Pao* faced difficulties and was forced to close down at the end of the year. Around the same time, the Penang Tongmenghui launched the *Kwong Wah Yit Poh*.

The idea of publishing the *Kwang Hwa Pao* or 'Glorious Chinese Newspaper' was originally conceived when Dr. Sun, Hu Hanmin, Huang Xing and Wang Jingwei visited

缅甸仰光光华报

Early committee of the Kwong Wah Yit Poh press.
Front, from right: Fang Qiu, Qiu Mingchang, Xie Cibian, Lin Fuquan. Back, from right: Xu Zhiyun, Lin Yibo, Chen Xinzheng, Lei Tieya, Chen Sandi.

Reproduced from The 70th Anniversary Commemorative Souvenir Magazine: Kwong Wah Yit Poh Press Berhad.

Penang in 1907. The plan was aborted when financial backing wavered due to a drop in tin prices.

The Rangoon Tongmenghui took up the idea and started the *Yan Kon Kwang Hwa Pao*. After a short run, the Rangoon paper was banned by the British colonial government due to its radical stand. Subsequently, the Rangoon Tongmenghui leader Zhuang Yin'an came to Penang and a committee was formed to revive the *Kwang Hwa Pao* as a daily paper.

Kwong Wah Yit Poh

Under Sun Yat Sen's guidance, the *Kwong Wah Yit Poh* was launched as a Chinese daily newspaper in Penang. The first issue was published on 2 December 1910 from the Tongmenghui Nanyang Headquarters at 120 Armenian Street. It became the Tongmenghui's main revolutionary organ in Malaya.

The initial set up for the newspaper was supervised by Hu Hanmin. Then Lei Tieya, who was recruited from Japan, came to Penang to serve as the first editor of the *Kwong Wah Yit Poh*. The newspaper provided jobs for Tongmenghui literati such as Dai Jitao who did short stints in the Nanyang.

Publication was almost interrupted due to financial problems, but at Zhuang Yin'an's suggestion, the *Kwong Wah Yit Poh* was converted into a public company. More than $10,000 was raised through the

Lei Tieya, the first editor

Dai Jitao, whose pen-name was Dai Tian Chou

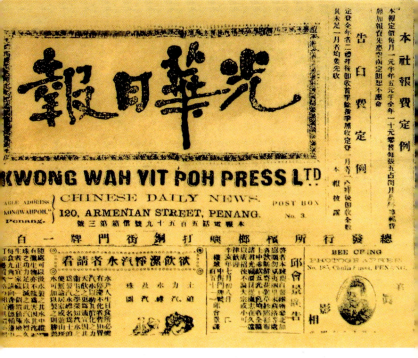

The calligraphy for the original *Kwong Wah Yit Poh* masthead was written by Lei Tieya, the first editor of the newspaper.

sale of public shares to re-capitalize the newspaper. An old printing machine of the *Zhang Quan Ri Bao* of Xiamen, which had been left behind in a private home in Penang, was acquired.

In the coming months, the *Kwong Wah Yit Poh* was to play an instrumental role in spreading awareness and raising funds for the revolution in China.

Sun Yat Sen stayed long enough to see the launch of the *Kwong Wah Yit Poh*, but had to leave Penang almost immediately after. He was expelled from Malaya and his expulsion dealt a severe blow to the revolutionary campaign.

Banished Again

The Governor of the Straits Settlements, Sir John Anderson, ordered Dr. Sun's banishment for having made 'an inflammatory speech in a Chinese club at Penang, inciting his hearers to support a revolution against the Manchu Dynasty.' On 26 November 1910, Dr. Sun wrote from Penang to his comrades in Singapore telling them he would travel to Europe and America, instead of going to Singapore for fundraising as planned.

Fortunately, the Nanyang fundraising effort has started well.... The Nanyang has no lack of enthusiastic people. All ordinary people who have any feelings will be moved by sincerity, even gold and stone can be shattered. As for those people who have helped out before, it does not necessarily mean that they have nothing to give this time; please tell them what we are facing right now and that it is not possible to delay. Indeed, all comrades should think of this as the campaign for the Last Battle.

The Complete Works of Sun Yat-sen, Vol. 1, *p. 499.*

Dr. Sun departed from Penang in early December on a German steamer, registered as a second class passenger. As he was worried that the Nanyang fundraising targets could not be met, he made up his mind to sail west and tap on his support in America.

Fundraising in Ipoh for the Second Guangzhou Uprising — those who had earlier taken part in the Penang Conference were Deng Zeru of Kuala Pilah (seated far left), Huang Xing (seated third from right) and Li Xiaozhang of Ipoh (standing second from right)

Reproduced from The Overseas Chinese and the 1911 Revolution.

By the time he came to live in Penang in 1910, Dr. Sun was already a wanted man in China, as well as *persona non grata* in Japan, French Indo-China, Dutch East Indies, Thailand and British Hong Kong. Conditions in Singapore were unfavourable due to heavy British surveillance and internal dissension within the Tongmenghui.

Penang was Dr. Sun's last stronghold in the region. After he was banished by the British colonial government of Malaya and Singapore, there was not a place left in the Nanyang where he was allowed to step foot.

Fundraising

After Sun Yat Sen's departure, Hu Hanmin, Huang Xing and Deng Zeru led the Nanyang fundraising campaign. The Tongmenghui members travelled to various towns and villages throughout Malaya to seek donations.

The first round of canvassing in Singapore, Melaka and Kuala Lumpur was disappointing, but a second round in the smaller towns of Seremban and Ipoh, Taiping and Kampar yielded better returns.

The Chinese in Singapore and Malaya contributed about one quarter of the total of $187,000 collected. The rest was raised from Chinese communities in Canada, the Dutch East Indies, French Indo-China, Thailand and the United States.

Money Raised in the Various Overseas Chinese Communities for the Second Guangzhou Uprising 1911	
Place	Sum of Money (Straits $ or HK$)
Canada	63,000
British Malaya & Singapore	47,663
Dutch East Indies	32,550
French Indo-China & Siam	30,423
United States of America	14,000
Total	187,636

Reproduced from The Overseas Chinese and the 1911 Revolution.

華僑革命史

惨人可也，在座遂捐得八千餘元。計越日趕收捐歘，孫先生一面遣派代表囘國接濟黨人，以作捲土重來之計；一面遣代表分途向各埠勸捐，以備資助軍需之用。黃克强、胡漢民曾到四州府鼓勵捐歘，成効甚佳。鄧澤如、鄭螺生、王源水、李孝章、丘怡領、蔡熾三、譚揚爲四州府最得力同志。譚揚曾變賣屋業數千元助軍需，更爲難能而可貴者。茲將余埠重要份子列下，此係憑予一己之憶力及根據民報出力壽歘者，倘有遺漏望爲指正，以便補錄。

瓜勝阜勝鄧澤如　芙蓉譚德棟　蔡熾三　黃心持　朱赤亮　林作舟吉
關帝應章等以文明閣德書報社民錄正張永福陳
楚楠　林義甸　潘兆鵬　鄧子瑜　楊伯文　沈聯芳　葉耀庭　陳進先　陳祥會
隆山丘怡領　陳占梅　佘鄭螺生　王源水　李孝章以新改良尚號鼓勵機
鳳紹丘羅顆　何悟里多　許子麟　何德如　黃吉辰　周献瑞仰光覺民書報社

十二

莊銀安　徐賚周　何蔭三　磯酒川　陳仲梼　鄧北熙　陳守金　陳植汀金陳玉着
張永福　林文曲　黃永田　曾宗曾　魏聲歐　陳鑑歷緬甸楊杜啓
仁瓦城振漢書報社楊承承到陳泰高緬甸咬墨趙澤圃吳榮聊太平林
翰泉陳志東古勞許瑞廷何雲皐亞齊士吉利曾文陳李鐵山麻坡劉
靜山岑東昔海何惠瓊亞勞邦土蘇逢春蘇松柏彭亨立早宋吉鳴實
突許福聊大巴東楊漢係加影楊穆勿瓜勝古毛黃愛基和豐張洪初
彭亨都拉沈訓胡啓蒙書報社彭亨星南鑒光巴央摹益
庐子貞曾順聊朱毛伍秋雨余寶王不顯拿乞鄧星南鑒光保誠秋資
書報社王月洲高又山廣益學堂萬里皐黃偉民智至書報社王植珊
端洛達通學校杜門葉競爭紅毛丹葉煩具務邊文明書報社黃屏伯
暗邦李耀南芙蓉知如華商書報社林澤南亞齊黃玉珊布先益
智書報社蔡卓南隆邦謝纘漢洹文丹丘守如楊劍虹籠島袁佈文積

丘嗣端黃泖坤綬純齋濤奕源林文琴徐洋溢柯清卓林貽博楊如金
許賣雲呑薛南黃長美蔡益敏徐積徐張仲彪凌榮枝潘漢倬許清江曾
受謝賜少品丘文紹陳台臬黃才擇陳迪安李慕參何建山崔鳳珊林
世安張祥陳陳統傳結堂謝此篤鄧紹權李鳳莚三謝四端殷阮生吳
逸像林鎰鐮陳傳統林文露朱益三端殷阮生有美王間黃蔡懷安桑有成林
伯度林博愛林光華洪周武顏子靈丘有美王間黃蔡懷安桑有成林
文遠丘新和黃坤松林華盛丘兆鵬蚋河涛鑾堡自立梁金盛陳民情鄧
光洪莊連勝謝文進周谷林楊少芬施惠聊何志林如瑞朱茂喬譚海版嘉
兆怡王鳴鳳林文一徐自如廣桂耀河咨呂益生理蔡長守脇宗漢謝丕郇吳成
寶沃沈瑞盜萬少聰張剛周達德陳河咨呂益生理蔡長守脇宗漢謝丕郇吳成
瑞璋天民社忠志尤澤燕謝生徐許生理蔡長守脇宗漢謝丕郇吳成
春鄭玉指李子崇周和瑣蔡益恭蔡水拱宋卜陳寬押當

華僑革命史

我菼曾賚柳甲調葉遇凡董裒余柏如吉礁陳榮林有祥高仟武勝
林玉桂通扣張珊珊日里民禮石廷良棉蘭桑瑞梯李增耀蘇英含葉
燕盛黃展展瑞波林子光張進輝謝芊崔水永山黃捷棻盧燈學高
煙劉柳村力忠公益書報社黃昌埕什武圣楚廷林錦莊浮爐山昔
句沈復權李巴巴閱書報社林幸福彭亨文多熊文初甲板謝八堯槟城
歐炳亮張鶴亭美利寶雪東新報發網濊環遠蕭佛波沙澄陸升如坤
虎社明新書社蔣報社社蔣報社民錄江沙覺民書報社薛木本伍
李月池藤香溢郭巴川洽沙用恭英周光集余齊國强學校直冬丁宜
公益書報社徐溢瓊震報振南黃文英丘開端開丹林明丘滄海洲水保
蘊山巴生顔福閱吳彩若林幸福彭亨文多熊文初甲板謝八堯槟城
報社熊升初巴閱書報社林葉僑敎育會江沙覺民書報社薛木本伍
黃金慶吳世榮丘兆鵬阮生有恭吳熊文初熊玉珊謝敬蔡古燈堂林如德

十三

Chen Xinzheng's list of the Malayan supporters who donated to the Second Guangzhou Uprising of 1911. As the original donors' list was burnt in 1915, Chen had to reconstruct this list from memory and newspaper records.

Reproduced from Chen Xinzheng Posthumous Collection.

Penang, 1890s. The Chinese opera was a favourite form of entertainment among the Chinese, rich and poor alike. It regularly attracted crowds of working-class labourers, the majority of whom enjoyed no family life here. The revolutionaries also used theatre to spread their ideas. Inspired by a Hong Kong revolutionary drama group that toured Malaya, a number of troupes were

formed locally, including the Jing Shi Ban (Warning of the Age Troupe) which was active in Penang in 1910. Performing for charity offered them some immunity from police interference. More than talks and publications, it was dramatic performances that reached the Chinese masses.

Chinese theatre performed in a coconut plantation, rural Penang, circa 1910. Tongmenghui members took advantage of such gatherings to spread their message and collect funds, even deep in the countryside. During the Xinhai Revolution of 1911, thousands of working-class Chinese, most of them recent migrants, volunteered to return to China and fight with the revolutionary armies.

Photograph courtesy of Geoffrey Wade

Memorial to the 72 Martyrs of Huanghuagang in Guangzhou (Canton).

Huanghua Gang Commemoration Park

REVOLUTION AND MARTYRDOM

The Second Guangzhou Uprising

For the 'Last Battle', Sun Yat Sen had mobilized all his supporters to give whatever they had. The Second Guangzhou Uprising, also called the 'Canton March 29 Uprising' was the most significant uprising ever organised by the Tongmenghui. Not only did it take place in Guangzhou, but many of the key players were sons of Guangdong province.

The plot reads like a script from a Hong Kong movie. Arms bought from several countries were secretly

Insurgents taken prisoner after the Second Guangzhou Uprising.

delivered to Canton. Forty clandestine cells were set up, each one working in isolation. Two rice shops were specially opened to provide safe meeting places. False couples organized weddings so that accommodation could be arranged for out-of-town 'wedding guests'. Weapons were smuggled to the scene in bridal palanquins carried on the shoulders of insurgents.

Huang Xing marched into Guangzhou with about 170 comrades, but luck was not with them. Intercepted by the authorities, the revolt was swiftly crushed by the Imperial Army. As reinforcements from Hong Kong arrived too late, many of the revolutionaries were killed or arrested.

Despite the terrible defeat, the Second Guangzhou Uprising achieved widespread fame. In Dr. Sun's estimation, 'the revolutionary spirits of the 72 Martyrs of the Huanghuagang Uprising shocked the whole world, and the circumstances already permit the success of the revolution.'

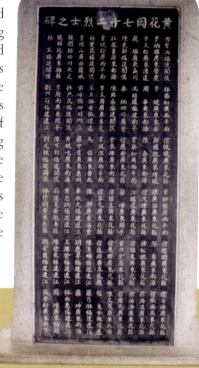

Stele at Huanghuagang with the names of the 72 Martyrs.

The Martyrs' Links with Penang

Tongmenghui comrades from all over Malaya gathered for a memorial service in honour of the Huanghuagang martyrs, held at Lin Rurui's estate, Penang.

The famous '72 martyrs' of the Second Guangzhou Uprising (officially 86 were executed) were later memorialized at the 'Yellow Flower Knoll', at Huanghuagang, Guangzhou.

Among those who sacrificed their lives were 'gifted poets, distinguished writers, popular journalists, skilled workers and farmers', including students who had recently returned from Japan.

At least 13 of the martyrs were recruited from Malaya and Singapore. Luo Zhonghuo hailed from Penang, while at least three other martyrs were sojourners who had embarked from Penang or spent time here.

The failure of the Second Guangzhou Uprising devastated the morale of the Penang supporters.

Luo Zhonghuo (1882—1911), of Kejia (Hakka) origin, from Hui Yang, Guangdong. A Penang-trained teacher who established a school in Kuala Lumpur; his poems and other writings inspired others to support the revolution.

Zhou Hua (Chiew Wah), of Guangdong (Cantonese) origin, a talented writer and secretary of the Tongmenghui Nanyang Headquarters in Singapore and Penang.

Chen Wenbao (1880—1911), of Kejia (Hakka) origin, from Dapu, Guangdong, who brought his family to Penang.

Li Yannan alias Sean, who sojourned as a wanted man to Penang and Burma. He was shot dead attacking the Governor's office during the uprising.

Shortly after the aborted uprising, Dr. Sun's Malayan supporters called at the Nanyang Headquarters and held a memorial service to mourn the fallen heros. Some revolutionaries who escaped narrowly with their lives were present to give eye-witness accounts of the tragic events.

The Xinhai Revolution

On 10 October 1911, the New Army in Wuchang revolted and seized power. After months of despondency, the Nanyang Headquarters in Penang was surprised to receive news of the Wuchang Uprising. They rose to the occasion and immediately dispatched $20,000 (Straits dollars) to Hong Kong to stabilize the revolutionary government.

The Wuchang Uprising marked the starting point of

Penang Philomatic Union members celebrating the capture of Wuhan province by the revolutionary armies during the Xinhai Revolution.

the Xinhai Revolution (named after the Xinhai year). Chinese provinces fell one after another to the revolutionary armies over a period of six weeks. Financial support from the Overseas Chinese was critical in consolidating the victories of the revolutionary forces.

The Role of the Nanyang Headquarters

In October 1911, Dr. Sun was in Denver, Colorado, when he received news about the success of the revolution. *En route* back to China, Dr. Sun broke voyage in Penang on 12 December 1911.

He was under strict surveillance by the British authorities, who advised him against making any 'public utterances' and escorted him to his residence at Dato' Kramat Road. He stayed in Penang for only a few hours, but managed to meet with his family and closest supporters.

Throughout the period of the Xinhai Revolution, that is, from October to December 1911, the Penang supporters put themselves at the service of the revolutionary forces. Some gave up their full time jobs or neglected their businesses to devote all their time to their duties at the Nanyang Headquarters. Telegrams, newspapers, a wide intelligence network and a constant flow of travellers, brought home the full force of events in China.

The Nanyang Headquarters was transformed into the nerve centre for the regional movement, helping to mobilize funds and recruits for the revolutionary forces. It received first-hand news about the revolution and disseminated the news by telegram to all the branches. The *Kwong Wah Yit Poh* whipped up public excitement by broadcasting the victories of the revolutionary government.

Branches and factions within the Tongmenghui, which had earlier slackened in their support for Dr.

Chinese Residency. Penang

The 'Five-Storey Villa' or Chinese Residency which belonged to Wu Shirong's father-in-law, Xie Deshun (Cheah Tek Soon). Wu persuaded his wife Xie Liumei (Cheah Liew Bee) to sell off the mansion to finance the revolution. The building was bought by Dai Xiyun (Tye Kee Yoon), Chinese Vice-Consul (1907-1911).

Postcard courtesy of Malcolm Wade.

Sun, now came forward to throw their weight behind the Xinhai Revolution. Sensing the tide of change, even the conservative Chinese turned around to back the winning side.

On 11 November 1911, the leaders of the Nanyang Headquarters called a public meeting at the Chinese Town Hall. It was attended by more than 1,000 people from all walks of life. A committee of 103 was formed, comprising representatives of every street in Penang, to organize house-to-house collections in urgent support of the revolution.

Wu Shirong was elected to represent the Overseas Chinese in Malaya, and to monitor all the funds sent to Hong Kong. He met up with Dr. Sun in China, in December that year.

The Chinese Republic Declared

Before the year was out, Sun Yat Sen was elected to head the new Chinese Republic, promptly declared on 1 January 1912. Almost the first thing Dr. Sun did as provisional president was to promulgate the adoption of the Western solar calendar (in place of the Chinese lunar calendar), and the abolition of the queue, a badge of Han Chinese servitude to the Manchus.

The Republican Revolution transformed the Chinese nation and the lives of ordinary Chinese in dramatic ways. Within a month of the Wuchang Uprising, more than 5,000 men in Penang had reportedly snipped off their queues. Then, on 16 December 1911, the Chinese Town Hall passed a resolution in a general meeting to affirm the abolition.

As the Penang Tongmenghui members were at the vanguard of the new hairstyle, the Malays living around Armenian Street called them *orang Cina potong tauchang* — 'the Chinese who cut off their queues'.

Certificate of appreciation, 1912, issued by Sun Yat Sen, as China's Provisional President, to the Penang Philomatic Union. A similar certificate was issued to the *Kwong Wah Yit Poh*.

'Penang. Chinese Boys' School'. This photograph actually shows a Singapore school, but the set-up of an early Chinese school in Penang would have looked remarkably similar. The tail worn by the Chinese was an object of ridicule to Westerners.
Postcard courtesy of Malcolm Wade.

As Manchu subjects all Chinese men, whether at home or abroad, were forced to shave their foreheads and keep a queue.

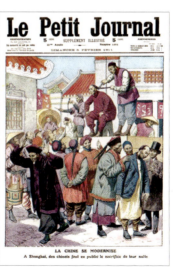

During the Xinhai Revolution, there was a widespread severing of queues among the Chinese, both voluntarily and by force.

Chen Cuifen

Sun Yat Sen's second wife. Madam Chen Cuifen was born in Xiamen, Fujian, in 1874. She died in Hong Kong in 1962 and was later reburied in the Sun family graveyard in Guangzhou. This portrait was photographed in Ipoh after the Revolution.

Courtesy of Foo Wan Thot.

DR. SUN'S FAMILY
IN PENANG

Dr. Sun's Residence in Penang

Dr. Sun Yat Sen's stay in Penang was one of the rare periods when most of the family was together for several months. Dr. Sun travelled to Penang on 19 July 1910. He was joined by his second wife Chen Cuifen in early August.

In September, Dr. Sun's elder brother Sun Mei was expelled from Hong Kong. As he had been looking after Dr. Sun's family in Hong Kong, he had no choice but to bring them to Penang. Sun Mei arrived in Penang — with Dr. Sun's first wife Madam Lu and his two daughters — in late October or early November, in time to attend the Penang Conference.

The only member of the family not with Dr. Sun was his eldest son, Sun Fo, who was studying in Honololu with the support of family friends in Hawai'i.

Madam Lu Muzhen, or Loo Muk Chen, was Sun Yat Sen's first wife. She was born in Guangdong in 1867 and died in Macao in 1952. She married Sun Yat Sen in May 1884. They had three children — a son, Sun Fo, and two daughters, Sun Yan and Sun Wan.

Museum of Dr. Sun Yat-Sen, Cuiheng.

Dr. Sun's family members who lived at 404 Dato' Kramat Road in 1910.

Lu Muzhen
aged 43

Sun Yan
aged 16

Sun Wan
aged 14

Chen Cuifen
aged 36

Sun Mei
aged 56

Dr. Sun Yat Sen
aged 44

Sun Mei alias Sun Dezhang, was Dr. Sun's elder brother. He was born in Cuiheng in 1854, and died in Macao in 1915. He became a successful businessman in Hawai'i and sponsored his brother's education there. Sun Mei spent his fortune backing Dr. Sun and the Chinese Revolution. In 1907, he filed for bankruptcy and left Hawai'i. After 1912, Sun Mei planned to return to Malaya to do some business, but his health failed him and he died soon afterward.

Museum of Dr. Sun Yat-Sen, Cuiheng.

Supporting The Family

Family picture taken in Hawai'i in 1903, with Dr. Sun's mother seated in the centre. *Museum of Dr. Sun Yat-Sen, Cuiheng.*

When Dr. Sun's family was living in Penang, they could not even afford to pay their monthly house rent of $20. The Penang supporters discussed Dr. Sun's situation and undertook to provide his family with $120 to $130 each month for their living expenses.

This stipend was borne by 11 members of the Penang Philomatic Union — Chen Xinzheng, Huang Jinqing, Wu Shirong, Qiu Mingchang, Pan Yiyuan, Qiu Kaiduan, Ke Qingzhuo, Xiong Yushan, Chen Shuzhai, Xie Yiqiao and Lu Wenhui.

While in Penang, Dr. Sun received news of his mother's death. As the Sun family was broke at the time, the Penang supporters collected donations for the funeral expenses.

Dr. Sun left Penang in December 1910, but his family stayed on until early 1912, maintained by Dr. Sun's friends. In a letter to his friend Deng Zeru in Siam on July 18, 1911, Dr. Sun wrote:

> *Now my family lives in Penang and the comrades there provide a hundred dollars for their living expenses every month. My two daughters are in school and when my wife gets sick, it is very hard for her to pay the medical expenses... It is true that it is hard to support a poor man for any length of time... I would like to ask you, if I may, to get together ten or twenty friends in towns other than Penang, and ask each of them to provide five or ten dollars monthly to help my family in Penang. The comrades in Penang have already helped for more than six months; they might be weary of the burden. I would appreciate it if this can be arranged...*
>
> The Complete Works of Sun Yat-sen, Vol. 1, *p. 526-527.*

Sun Yat Sen's wives and daughters, Madam Chen Cuifen, Madam Lu Muzhen, Sun Yan and Sun Wan (front row, 7th, 8th, 9th, and 10th from left). The photo was taken in Singapore in February 1912, when the family was travelling to China to be reunited with Dr. Sun after the revolution.

Two Letters to Mrs. Cantlie

In November 1910, Dr. Sun wrote two letters to Mrs. Cantlie, the wife of his mentor Dr. James Cantlie, in London. The first letter was dated 20 November, and the second one, 24 November; both were signed 'Y.S.Sun'. Between the time of writing these two letters, Dr. Sun had a drastic change of plans, and had to leave his family behind in Penang.

From Sun Yat Sen, Penang, to Mrs. Cantlie, London, November 20, 1910.

I am very busy recently, indeed there are good many things to be done in China, and I could not say definitely when I could pay another visit to England and shall have the pleasure to meet you again there.

My family is with me here now, but my son is still study [sic] at Honolulu...

Sun Yat Sen's letters to Mrs. Cantlie. Source: Wellcome Library, London.

Penang, November 24, 1910.

My dear Mrs Cantlie:—

I have posted a letter to you just a few days ago, then I had not the least idea of coming to England so soon. But now I am wanting to go to England and America to do some business. I shall sail in a fortnight of time, and expect to see you soon in London. Please keep my coming secret from the Chinese Legation.

In case any one come to your house to enquire me in the name of Chungsan before my arrival that man will be a friend of mine you may treat him so.

With kindest regards to you and the Doctor

Very truly yours

Y.S. Sun

From Sun Yat Sen, Penang, to Mrs. Cantlie, London, November 24, 1910

I have posted a letter to you just a few days ago, then I had not the least idea of coming to England so soon. But now I am wanting to go to England and America to do some business. I shall sail in a fortnight of time, and expect to see you soon in London. Please keep my coming secret from the China Legation.

In case any one come to your house to enquire me in the name of Chungsan before my arrival that man will be a friend of mine you may treat him so.

A Letter To His Two Daughters

Sun Yan (right), born in Cuiheng, 1894, died at the age of 19 in Macao. Sun Wan (left), born in Honolulu, 1896, died in Macao, 1979. Dr. Sun's two daughters spent more than a year growing up in Penang, where they attended English-medium school. Here, they spent precious time with their father, who was usually away making revolution.

Museum of Dr. Sun Yat-Sen, Cuiheng.

Sun Yan, Sun Wan and their brother Sun Fo in Nanjing in 1912. When the sisters were in Penang — between late 1910 and early 1912 — their brother was in Honolulu.

Opposite: Letter dated 20 December 1910, from Dr. Sun to his two daughters, written just after he was banished, on the voyage from Penang to Europe.

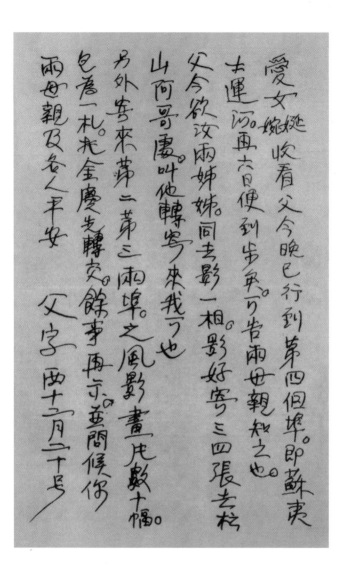

My dear daughters, Yan, Wan, to receive and view. Tonight, your father has already reached the fourth port of call, the Suez Canal. In another six days I will arrive in England. Please inform your two mothers. Now, father would like both of you sisters to take a group photo together. After that, send two or three pieces to your brother's place in Honolulu. Ask him to forward them to me. One more thing, I have sent the scenery photographs of the second and third ports of call — several dozens of them — in a package. I have asked (Huang) Jinqing to forward them, the rest I will show you later. Also send my regards to your two mothers and everyone, and inform them that I am safe. From your father.

Chen Cuifen

Two portraits of Chen Cuifen: with Dr. Sun, and with Sun Mei's grandson Sun Qian in Hongkong, 1912.

Museum of Dr. Sun Yat-Sen, Cuiheng.

Chen Cuifen met Dr. Sun at the age of 17, and was his constant companion during his years in exile. She not only helped Dr. Sun in his daily routine but was also involved in risky activities such as carrying secret messages or smuggling firearms.

As Dr. Sun's second wife, she got along with his first wife Madam Lu; they treated each other like sisters. Dr. Sun's children called Chen Cuifen 'second mother'. Years later, after Dr. Sun remarried, the descendants would refer to Madam Lu as 'Au-men Po' (Macau wife), Chen Cuifen as 'Nanyang Po' (Southeast Asian wife) and Song Qingling as 'Shanghai Po' (Shanghai wife).

In August 1910, Chen Cuifen arrived in Penang to join Dr. Sun. She did the housekeeping, cooking and laundry for Dr. Sun's family and fellow revolutionaries. After Dr. Sun was banished from Malaya, Chen Cuifen went down to Ipoh as his representative to raise funds for the Revolution.

In February 1912, she travelled to China with Madam Lu and her two daughters; while the others went on to join Dr. Sun, Chen Cuifen stayed back in Macao. She kept two precious gifts from Dr. Sun — her wedding ring and his watch, originally a gift from his mentor Dr. James Cantlie.

A year or two later, Chen Cuifen returned to Malaya. She was sent ahead by Sun Mei to explore business possibilities in Malaya. She lived in Penang, Taiping and Ipoh, and adopted a daughter Su Zhongying who later married Sun Mei's grandson, Sun Qian; the couple's second child was born in Ipoh.

Chen Cuifen and Dr. Sun's two daughters, in Ipoh on a fundraising mission.

Courtesy of Foo Wan Thot.

THE LEGACY OF SUN YET SEN'S SUPPORTERS IN PENANG

The *Kwong Wah Yit Poh* newspaper bureau at 16 Malay Street.

Courtesy of Kwong Wah Yit Poh Press Berhad.

After The Revolution

Released during the Xinhai Revolution, Wang Jingwei (middle) was in Penang on his way to Europe in 1912. Welcoming him were Huang Jinqing, Wu Shirong, Xiong Yushan (seated 2nd, 4th and 5th from left), Chen Xinzheng and Qiu Mingchang (standing 2nd and 3rd from left).

After the Xinhai Revolution, the Tongmenghui party was superseded by the Guomindang (Kuomintang), which set up branches all over Malaya.

The Penang Philomatic Union, which still served as the Tongmenghui Nanyang Headquarters, moved to 52A Queen Street on 29 January 1912.

On 1 February 1913, the *Kwong Wah Yit Poh* and the Penang Philomatic Union moved into 16 and 18 Malay Street, respectively. The Philomatic Union then bought over the Chinese Merchants Club (Xiao Lan Ting) at 65 Macalister Road and has been based there since 1917.

Dr. Sun's supporters were at the forefront of the movement for modern Chinese education in Penang, establishing schools such as the Chung San Primary School, Bayan Lepas (1912), Chung Ling School (1917) and Fukien Girls' School (1920), subsequently called the Penang Chinese Girls' School.

After 1911, the *Kwong Wah Yit Poh* was run by the Guomindang party in Malaya but became independent in the 1950s. Today, it is one of the oldest Chinese newspapers in the world.

The Fukien Girls' School in the Penang Philomatic Society building.
Reproduced from Historical Personalities of Penang.

Memorial tribute to Chen Xinzheng (died 1924), founder of Chung Ling High School. The school was then occupying the Penang Philomatic Society building at Macalister Road.

Reproduced from Chen Xinzheng Posthumous Collection.

Map of George Town, Penang, circa 1920, showing road networks and tram routes.

Reproduced from An Official Guide to Eastern Asia. Source: Cornell University Library, Southeast Asia Visions Collection.

Sites Associated with Sun Yat Sen and his Penang Supporters

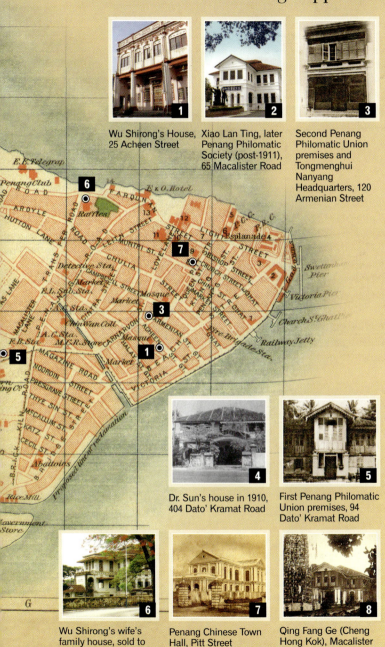

1. Wu Shirong's House, 25 Acheen Street
2. Xiao Lan Ting, later Penang Philomatic Society (post-1911), 65 Macalister Road
3. Second Penang Philomatic Union premises and Tongmenghui Nanyang Headquarters, 120 Armenian Street
4. Dr. Sun's house in 1910, 404 Dato' Kramat Road
5. First Penang Philomatic Union premises, 94 Dato' Kramat Road
6. Wu Shirong's wife's family house, sold to finance the Revolution, Northam Road
7. Penang Chinese Town Hall, Pitt Street
8. Qing Fang Ge (Cheng Hong Kok), Macalister Road

Location of 120 Armenian Street

The Penang Philomatic Union and the Tongmenghui Nanyang Headquarters were located at 120 Armenian Street. From here, it was a short walk to Wu Shirong's house on Acheen Street and Huang Jinqing's office at Beach Street.

The Hokkiens called the street *'Phah tang ke'* (Cantonese, *Ta thung kai*) or 'striking copper street', after the Malay brazier's shop across the road from 120 Armenian Street. The curved, narrow street traverses a multi-ethnic neighbourhood, with many small alleys and secret gateways leading to temple courtyards and mosque compounds. Secret societies, which famously instigated the Penang Riots in 1867, were entrenched in this area until their prohibition in 1890.

Reproduced from Wadah Tumpuan Warisan Budaya *brochure.*

The Penang Philomatic Union at 120 Armenian Street provided a good escape route. In case of raids, the revolutionaries could easily slip away from the back of the house into the Tamil Muslim enclaves of Kampong Kolam and Kampong Kaka.

George Town Survey Map, 1893

A Note on the Penang Sites

Secrecy, anonymity and mobility were important considerations for the Tongmenghui in choosing the locations of their bases.

It appears that the Tongmenghui sites had certain things in common. They had easy access to the tramline, river transport, the railway station and the harbour. Secondly, the premises were strategically positioned with a great variety of pedestrian approaches. Thirdly, they were located in mixed ethnic areas, in close proximity to informal Malay-Muslim settlements — all the better to slip in and out undetected by suspicious Chinese neighbours.

Instead of formal street names, the Chinese in Penang habitually used local place names. For example, Dr. Sun's mailing address in Penang was Huang Jinqing's shop 'Tek Cheang', located along a section of Beach Street, with the local Hokkien place name of *Tuan Lo-sin* (Cantonese, *Tuan Lo-san*). This section, lined with Chinese import-export companies, between Acheen and Armenian Streets, was named after 'Tuan Hussain' or Tengku Syed Hussain who once owned most of the houses here. From the shop, it was a three-minute walk to the tramline and clan jetties along Weld Quay.

The first address of the Penang Philomatic Union was at Dato' Kramat Road, called *Kam-a-hui* (Cantonese, *Kam chai-un*) or 'orange grove'. Dato' Kramat Road was a peri-urban area surrounded by Malay settlements and fruit orchards.

Sun Yat Sen's house, at 404 Dato' Kramat Road, was located at a particular section of Dato' Kramat Road called *Si-kham tiam* (Cantonese, *Si kan-tim*) — meaning 'four shops'. This was the section between the Dato' Kramat Police Station and the Prison. About three minutes' walk from Dr. Sun's house was 'Dato' Kramat Garden', also called 'Brown Gardens', a public park where Dr. Sun would have enjoyed his morning or evening strolls.

The Ayer Itam—Jetty tramline connected Wu Shirong's Swee Hock Hui (Rui Fu Yuan) and the houses along Dato' Kramat Road to the town centre, harbour and railway.

The tram coming from Dato' Kramat Road. Penang was the first town in Malaysia to introduce municipal electrical supply in 1904 and the tram service in 1906. Dr. Sun, who enjoyed modern things, was probably a frequent rider on the Penang tram!

Postcard courtesy of Malcolm Wade.

Rickshaws plying Campbell Street – Penang's main shopping and entertainment district for the Chinese. Along this street were barbers, tailors, shops selling medicines, textiles, shoes, watches, as well as Chinese theatres, liquor stores, opium dens, brothels and pawnshops.

Campbell Street, Penang, circa 1920.

Postcard courtesy of Malcolm Wade.

120 ARMENIAN STREET
THEN AND NOW

Ownership of 120 Armenian Street

1875—1900

The earliest document relating to 120 Armenian Street dates from 1875. The first owner was Cheah Joo Seang, most likely the Hokkien leader who was a trustee of the Cheah Kongsi from 1879 to 1891.

Indenture of 1900 conveying the property to Lim Boon Yeow

Lim's signature

1900—1913

The house belonged to 'Lim Boon Yeow of Pitt Street Penang Trader'. In 1909 it became the premises of the Penang Philomatic Union and the Penang branch of the Tongmenghui.

From 1910, the *Kwong Wah Yit Poh* was published from this address. The Tongmenghui moved out in January 1912, and the *Kwong Wah Yit Poh* press in 1913.

The calligraphic plaque presented to Lim Boon Yeow in 1900 as a house-warming gift.

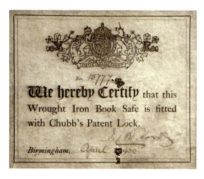

This iron book safe might have been used by the Penang Tongmenghui to store their cash and documents. Manufactured in Birmingham in 1900, the safe is certified fireproof and secured by a 'Chubb's patent lock'.

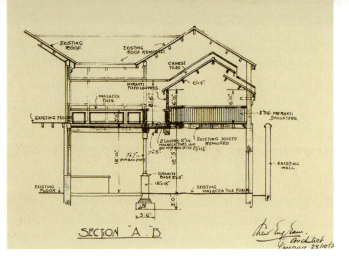

1913—1926

The house was sold to three women from Carnarvon Street — widows Puah Gek Thuan and Puah Gek Sim, and a married woman Puah Gek Soke. In 1924, Madam Phuah Gek Tuan commissioned the architect Chew Eng Eam to make alterations to the kitchen area, most likely in response to the backyard being given up for a new road, Kampong Kolam. It was probably during Madam Phuah's time that the house was refurbished — the staircase was relocated, wall cupboards were installed facing the air well, and the floor was relaid with patterned cement tiles.

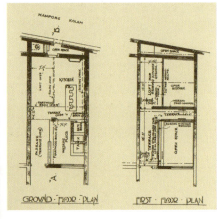

Left: The staircase.
Top and above: Kitchen alteration plans of 1924 by Chew Eng Eam.

The air-well is an attractive feature of the tropical shophouse, allowing light and ventilation to flood the interior of a long and narrow building. The atrium space illuminates the second hall.

Left: Ch'ng Teong Swee's company sign.
Below: Ch'ng Teong Swee and his first wife.
Left below: Nyonya matriarch Tan Ean Siew

1926—1993

The house was owned by a merchant Ch'ng Teong Swee. He used it as a family residence. His stepmother Madam Tan Ean Siew, who made Nyonya cakes for weddings, was the matriarch of the house. After the Japanese Occupation, in 1945, the family firm Ch'ng Eng Joo was re-started here before moving to Chulia Street. In 1993, the house was purchased by the author's family.

Above: The ornamental wooden screen and family altar. Today, the front hall displays a pictorial exhibition on Dr. Sun Yat Sen in Penang.
Far left: The kitchen with an original firewood stove used by Madam Tan to make Nyonya cakes.
Left: The back airwell which adjoins the kitchen.

Visit by Dignitaries

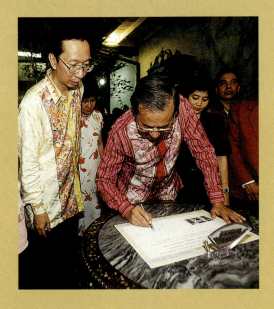

The first 'Dr. Sun Yat Sen in Penang' exhibition, inaugurated by Dato' Seri (now Tun) Dr. Mahathir Mohamed, then Malaysian Prime Minister, in conjunction with the first national Chinese New Year Open House in Penang in 2001. He was accompanied by the then Deputy Prime Minister, Dato' Seri Abdullah Ahmad Badawi (now the Prime Minister) and the former Penang Chief Minister Tan Sri Dr. Koh Tsu Koon.

Mr. Hu Jintao, the President of China (then vice-president) visiting 120 Armenian Street in April 2002.

Courtesy of Xinhua News Agency

Visit by Mr. Wu Bangguo, China's National People's Congress standing committee chairman, 2005.

SUN YAT SEN IN PENANG

A scene from the movie *Road To Dawn* (2007), about Sun Yat Sen (acted by Winston Chao) in Penang. The Penang Conference was re-enacted at 120 Armenian Street, the venue where Dr. Sun made his famous speech to raise funds for the Second Guangzhou Uprising.

The movie, which was shot entirely on location in Penang, won the Hua Biao Award for Most Outstanding Newcomer Scriptwriter (Maezi), Shanghai International Film Festival Media Awards for Best Actor (Winston Chao) and Most Promising Newcomer (Wu Yue), and the Golden Angel award at the Chinese American Film Festival.

Courtesy of the movie Road To Dawn.

Chronology

1906. Sun Yat Sen made his first trip to Penang where he was put up at the Xiao Lan Ting club. He gave a dinner speech to the club members about San Min Zhuyi and how China would fall if they did not overthrow the Manchu regime.

The Tongmenghui Penang branch was formed with 22 members, electing Wu Shirong as founding chairman and Huang Jinqing as deputy chairman.

Early 1907. Sun Yat Sen, Hu Hanmin, Huang Xing and Wang Jingwei gave public speeches at the Penang Chinese Town Hall. Dr. Sun's talk was entitled 'The Overthrow of the Manchus is the Prerequisite for Saving China.'

While in Penang, Huang Xing issued a pamphlet urging the Han Chinese to reject the Manchu queue.

Early 1908. Soon after the failure of the Zhennanguan Uprising (in December 1907), Chen Xinzheng invited Wang Jingwei to give a talk at San Shan Club. His talk was entitled 'The Fujian compatriots must particularly help the Revolution.'

1908, probably May. After being expelled from Tongking (in March 1908), Sun Yat Sen came to stay at Lin Zisheng's place at *Sar Kak Chan* (near Victoria Green). They received good news about the Hekou Uprising in Yunnan, but the success was short-lived.

Sun Yat Sen gave a public talk at the Xiao Lan Ting Club entitled 'China will be conquered if the Manchus are not overthrown'.

Late 1908. Wu Shirong called a meeting at Rui Fu Yuan to start a reading club.

Penang Philomatic Union family day, 1910.

6 December 1908. The Penang Philomatic Union was formed at a public meeting at the Penang Chinese Town Hall.

31 January 1909. The Penang Philomatic Union was inaugurated at 94 Dato' Kramat Road.

23 May 1909. The Penang Philomatic Union moved to 120 Armenian Street.

1909. Wang Jingwei gave a public talk at the Xiao Lan Ting Club, Penang, entitled 'Revolution is the only answer to advance China's commerce'.

February 1910. Mutiny of the Cantonese New Army in Guangzhou, headed by Zhao Sheng.

11 July 1910. Dr. Sun arrived in Singapore from Japan.

20 July 1910. Dr. Sun came to Penang and stayed for over four months.

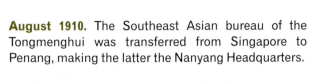

August 1910. The Southeast Asian bureau of the Tongmenghui was transferred from Singapore to Penang, making the latter the Nanyang Headquarters.

Dr. Sun reorganized the party under the new name Zhonghua Geming Dang (Chinese Revolutionary Party).

13 November 1910. Dr. Sun chaired a secret regional meeting of the Tongmenghui at 404 Dato' Kramat Road to plan the Second Guangzhou Uprising; this became known as the 'Penang Conference' (Bineng Huiyi).

14 November 1910. Dr. Sun chaired an Emergency Meeting at the Tongmenghui Nanyang Headquarters, 120 Armenian Street, and launched the fundraising campaign for the Second Guangzhou Uprising.

2 December 1910. The first issue of the *Kwong Wah Yit Poh* was published from 120 Armenian Street, Penang.

6 or 7 December, 1910. Dr. Sun left Penang as a result of being banished.

27 April 1911. The Second Guangzhou Uprising was bravely staged by the Tongmenghui. It was also called the 'Canton March 29 Uprising' as it took place on the 29th day of the 3rd month of the Chinese lunar calendar.

Some weeks later, the Tongmenghui met at Lin Rurui's estate house to mourn the martyrs.

10 October 1911. The Wuchang Uprising, also called the 'Double Tenth' Uprising, broke out.

11 November 1911. A public meeting was held at the Penang Chinese Town Hall to show support for the revolution.

12 December 1911. Dr. Sun stopped in Penang for the last time, *en route* to China.

A poster with a portrait of Sun Yat Sen and his last will and testament, as transcribed by Wang Jingwei. Before the Japanese Occupation, Chinese school students in Malaya had to bow before Dr. Sun's portrait and recite his will by heart during school assembly.

16 December 1911. The Penang Chinese Town Hall passed a resolution to abolish the queue.

1 January 1912. The Republic of China was inaugurated, with Dr. Sun as the first Provisional President.

Bibliography

Publications

Bergere, Marie-Claire. *Sun Yat-sen*. Trans. Janet Lloyd. Stanford: Stanford University Press, 1998.

Calligraphy Treasures of Zhongshan Committee 中山墨宝编委会, ed. *Calligraphy Treasures of Zhongshan*, Vol. 6: Correspondences, Part 1 《中山墨宝・第六卷・书信（上）》. Beijing: Beijing Publishing House, 1996.

Center of Chinese History Studies, Guangdong Academy of Social Sciences, et al 广东省社会科学院历史研究室等, eds. *The Complete Works of Sun Yat-sen*, Vol. 1: Letters, 1890-1911《孙中山全集・第1卷・书信1890－1911》. Beijing: Zhonghua Bookshop, 1981.

Chen Xinzheng 陈新政. 'A History of the Overseas Chinese Involvement in the Chinese Revolution' 《华侨革命史》. *Chen Xinzheng Posthumous Collection* 《陈新政遗集》. Undated.

Dr. Sun Yat-sen Museum 孙中山纪念馆, ed. *Dr. Sun Yat-sen Museum Exhibition Catalogue*《孙中山纪念馆展览图录》. Hong Kong: Dr. Sun Yat-sen Museum, 2006.

Historical Personalities of Penang Committee. *Historical Personalities of Penang*. Penang: Penang Museum, 1986.

Kwong Wah Yit Poh 光华日报. *70th Anniversary Commemorative Souvenir Magazine, 1910-1980* 《光华日报七十周年纪念特刊》. Penang: Kwong Wah Yit Poh Press Berhad, 1980.

Lee, Kam Hing and Chow Mun Seong. *Biographical Dictionary of the Chinese in Malaysia*. Petaling Jaya, Selangor, Malaysia: Pelanduk Publications, 1997.

Lee, Tai To, ed. *The 1911 Revolution: The Chinese in British and Dutch Southeast Asia*. Singapore: Heinemann Publishers Asia, 1987.

Leo, Suryadinata 廖建裕. 'Tongmenghui, Sun Yat Sen and the Chinese in Southeast Asia: A Revisit' 《同盟会、孙中山与东南亚华人》. Singapore: Chinese Heritage Centre, 2006.

Lo, Mun Yu. 'Chinese Names of Streets in Penang.' *Journal of the Straits Branch of the Royal Asiatic Society*, Vol. 33, 1900.

Lum, Yansheng Ma and Raymond Mun Kong Lum. *Sun Yat-sen in Hawaii: Activities and Supporters*. Honolulu: Hawaii Chinese History Centre and Dr. Sun Yat-sen Hawaii Foundation, 1999.

Shanghai Museum of Sun Yat-sen's Former Residence 上海孙中山故居纪念馆, ed. *A Photo Album of Sun Yat-sen in Macau*《孙中山与澳门图集》. Shanghai: Shanghai People's Publishing House, 1999.

Sun, Lily Sui-fong 孙穗芳, ed. *An Album In Memory of Dr. Sun Yat-sen: A Great Man and Epoch-maker*《我的祖父孙中山先生纪念集：一位开创世纪奇迹的伟人》. Nanjing: Nanjing University Press, 2001.

Teoh Shiaw Khuan 张少宽. *Penang Conference & the 1911 Chinese*

Revolution: How Dr. Sun Yat Sen Plotted to Change Chinese History 《孙中山与庇能会议：策动广州三二九之役》. Penang: Nanyang Field Studies, 2004.

The Department of Railways, Tokyo. *An Official Guide to Eastern Asia: Trans-continental Connections between Europe & Asia*, Vol. 5: East Indies, including Philippine Islands, French Indo-China, Siam, Malay Peninsula and Dutch East Indies, 2nd ed. Tokyo: The Department of Railways, 1920. Source: Southeast Asia Visions Collection, Cornell University Library.

The Museum of Dr. Sun Yat-Sen, Cuiheng 孙中山故居纪念馆. *The Relatives and Descendants of Dr. Sun Yat-Sen* 《孙中山的亲属与后裔》. Beijing: Encyclopedia of China Publishing House, 2001.

Wang, Gungwu. *Community and Nation: Essays on Southeast Asia and the Chinese*. Singapore: Heinemann Educational Books Asia Ltd, 1981.

The Souvenir of the 30th Anniversary of the Penang Philomatic Union 《槟城阅书报社卅周年纪念特刊》. Penang: Penang Philomatic Union, 1938.

Yang Hanxiang 杨汉翔. 'The speeches of the President in Penang pertaining to the Planning of the 1911 Canton Uprising' 《纪总理庚戌在槟城关于筹划辛亥广州举义之演说》. *Historical Materials Pertaining to the 1911 Chinese Revolution*, Vol. II 《辛亥革命史料选辑（续编）》. Ed. Qiu Quanzheng 丘权政 and Du Chunhe 杜春和. Changsha, Hunan, China: Hunan People's Publishing House, 1983. 101-103. Originally published in *Nation Building Monthly* 《建国月刊》, Vol. 3, No. 1, May 1930. The excerpts are translated by Tan Yau Chong.

Yen, Ching-hwang. *Community and Politics: The Chinese in Colonial Singapore and Malaysia*. Singapore: Times Academic Press, 1995.

____*The Overseas Chinese and the 1911 Revolution: With Special Reference to Singapore and Malaya*. Kuala Lumpur: Oxford University Press, 1976.

Yong, C.F. and R.B. McKenna. *The Kuomintang Movement in British Malaya, 1912-1949*. Singapore: Singapore University Press, 1990.

Exhibition
Exhibition on Sun Yat Sen in Penang, 2001 at 120 Armenian Street, Penang. Chinese text by Ong Seng Huat; English text by Khoo Salma Nasution based on research by Ong Seng Huat, with additional inputs by Goh Mai Loon and Lim Gaik Siang.

Institutional Sources
Dr. Sun Yat-sen Museum, Hong Kong
Kwong Wah Yit Poh Press Berhad, Penang
Museum of Dr. Sun Yat-sen, Cuiheng, China.
Southeast Asia Visions Collection, Cornell University Library, Ithaca
Sun Yat Sen Nanyang Memorial Hall, Singapore
Wellcome Library, London

Websites
Huanghua Gang Commemoration Park *http://www.72martyrs.com.cn*
Sun Yat Sen Nanyang Memorial Hall *http://www.wanqingyuan.com.sg*

Glossary

Acheen Street　打石街

Bincheng Yueshu Baoshe　槟城阅书报社

Bineng Huiyi　庇能会议

Ch'ng Eng Joo　庄荣裕

Ch'ng Teong Swee　庄忠水

Chaozhou　潮州

Cheah Joo Seang　谢裕生

Cheah Liew Bee　谢柳美

Chee Swee Ling　徐瑞霖

Chen Bijun　陈璧君

Chen Cuifen　陈翠芬

Chen Shuzhai　陈述斋

Chen Wenbao　陈文褒

Chen Xinzheng　陈新政

Cheng Hong Kok　清芳阁

Cheong Fatt Tze　张弼士

Chew Eng Eam　周荣炎

Chiew Wah　周华

Chinese Revolutionary Party　中华革命党

Chong Shing Yit Pao　中兴日报

Choong Cheng Kean　庄清建

Chung Ling School　钟灵学校

Chung San Primary School　中山小学

Cuiheng　翠亨村

Dabu　大埔

Dai Jitao　戴季陶

Danzhou　儋州

Deng Zeru　邓泽如

Fujian　福建

Fukien Girls' School　福建女学校

Goh Say Eng　吴世荣

Gong Yi　公益

Guangdong　广东

Guangxu, Emperor　光绪皇帝

Guomindang　国民党

Hainan　海南

Hakka　客家

Hokkien　福建

Hu Hanmin　胡汉民

Hua Ch'iao　华侨

Huang Jinqing　黄金庆

Huang Xing　黄兴

Huanghuagang　黄花岗

Hui Yang　惠阳

Jing Shi Ban　警世班

Kam-a hui　柑仔园

Ke Qingzhuo　柯清倬

Kejia　客家

Kong Hock Keong　广福宫

Kuan Yim Teng　观音亭

Kuomintang　国民党

Kwong Wah Jit Poh　光华日报

Lei Tieya　雷铁崖

Li Xiaozhang　李孝章

Li Yannan　李雁南

Li Yixia　李义侠

Lim Boon Yeow　林文耀

Lin Rurui　林如瑞

Lin Shi'an　林世安

Lin Wenyao　林文耀

Lin Zhisheng　林紫盛

Loo Muk Chen　卢慕贞

Lu Wenhui　陆文辉

Luo Zhonghuo　罗仲霍

Mao Zedong　毛泽东

Min Bao　民报

Minnanhua　闽南话

Nakayama　中山

Nanyang　南洋

Ng Kim Kheng　黄金庆

Pan Yiyuan　潘奕源

Penang Chinese Chamber of Commerce　槟榔屿中华总商会

Penang Philomatic Union　槟城阅书报社

Penang Sin Poe　槟城新报

Penang　槟榔屿／槟城

Phah tang ke　打铜仔街

Ping Zhang Gong Guan　平章公馆

Puah Gek Thuan　潘玉端

Puah Gek Sim　潘玉心

Puah Gek Soke　潘玉淑

Qing　清

Qiu Kaiduan　丘开端

Qiu Mingchang　丘明昶

San Min Zhuyi　三民主义

San Shan Club　三山公所

Second Guangzhou Uprising　第二次广州起义

Si-kham tiam　四坎店

Sun Dezhang　孙德彰

Sun Mei   孙眉
Sun Qian   孙乾
Sun Wan   孙婉
Sun Wen   孙文
Sun Yan   孙娫
Sun Yat Sen   孙逸仙
Sun Zhongshan   孙中山
Tan Ean Siew   陈燕秀
Tek Cheang   得昌号
Teochew   潮州
Thio Tiaw Siat   张肇燮
Three People's Principles   三民主义
Tongmenghui   同盟会
Tuan Lo-sin   缎罗申
Tye Kee Yoon   戴喜云
Wan Qing Yuan   晚晴园
Wang Jingwei   汪精卫
Wei Xin   维新
Winston Chao   赵文瑄
Wu Shirong   吴世荣
Wu Zhihui   吴稚晖
Wuchang Uprising   武昌起义
Xiao Lan Ting   小兰亭
Xie Yiqiao   谢逸桥
Xing Zhong Hui   兴中会
Xinhai   辛亥
Xiong Yushan   熊玉珊
Xu Ruilin   徐瑞霖
Yan Kon Kwang Hwa Pao   仰光光华报
Yang Hanxiang   杨汉翔
Zhang Quan Ribao   漳泉日报
Zhao Boxian   赵伯先
Zhao Sheng   赵声
Zheng Chenggong   郑成功
Zhong Hua   中华
Zhongguo Tongmenghui   中国同盟会
Zhonghua Geming Dang   中华革命党
Zhou Hua   周华
Zhuang Yin'an   庄银安
Zhuang Qingjian   庄清建

Index

Cantlie, James 13, 88-89
Ch'ng Teong Swee 114
Cheah Joo Seang 110
Chen Bijun 27
Chen Cuifen 82, 84-85, 87, 92-93
Chen Wenbao 75
Chen Xinzheng 37, 41, 48, 59, 65, 86, 96, 99, 120
Chinese Chamber of Commerce, Penang 23
Chinese Town Hall, Penang 21, 28, 34-37, 79-81, 101, 120-123
Chong Shing Yit Pao 58
Chung Ling School 41, 97-99
Chung San Primary School 97

Dai Jitao 60
Deng Zeru 50, 63-64, 87

Emergency Meeting 52-55, 122

Fukien Girls' School 41, 97

Guomindang 96-97

Hu Hanmin 26, 34, 50, 58, 60, 64, 120
Huang Jinqing 34, 37-38, 40-41, 46, 48, 50, 86, 91, 96, 102, 104, 120
Huang Xing 26, 34, 50, 58, 63-64, 73, 120
Huanghuagang 70-71, 73-74

John Anderson, Governor of Straits Settlements 62

Kwang Hwa Pao 58-59
Kwong Wah Yit Poh 58-61, 78, 80, 94-97, 111, 122

Lei Tieya 59-60
Li Xiaozhang 50, 63
Li Yannan 75
Li Yixia 50
Lim Boon Yeow 110-111
Lin Rurui 74, 122
Lin Shi'an 38, 50
Lin Zisheng 36, 37, 120
Lu Muzhen 84-85, 87, 92-93
Luo Zhonghuo 74-75

Minpao Magazine 26-27, 58
Nanyang Headquarters 14, 47-49, 52-53, 55, 60, 75-76, 78-79, 96, 101-102, 122

Penang Conference 50-51, 56, 63, 122
Penang Philomatic Union 36-41, 76-77, 80, 96- 99, 101-104, 110, 121
Penang Sin Poe 56-58
Phua Gek Thuan 112
Pinang Gazette 56

Qing Fang Ge 22, 56-57, 101
Qiu Minchang 37, 41, 48, 59, 86, 96

Road To Dawn 118-119
Rui Fu Yuan 36, 120

San Shan Club 29, 120
Second Guangzhou Uprising 50, 52-53, 72-75, 122
Song Qingling 92
Straits Echo 56-57
Sun Fo 84, 90
Sun Mei 12, 50, 84-85, 93
Sun Qian 92-93
Sun Wan 85-87, 90-91, 93
Sun Yan 85-87, 90-91, 93
Su Zhongying 93

Tongmenghui 14-15, 26-27, 36-41, 46-50, 58-59, 69, 72, 74-75, 80, 96, 104, 106, 110-111, 120, 122

Wan Qing Yuan 14, 16-17
Wang Jingwei 26-27, 29, 34-36, 40, 47, 58, 96, 120-121, 123
Wu Shirong 23, 30-31, 34, 36-37, 40-41, 46, 48, 50, 56, 79, 86, 96, 101-102, 105, 120
Wu Zhihui 47, 49
Wuchang Uprising 27, 76, 80, 122

Xiao Lan Ting 34, 97, 101, 120
Xin Zhong Hui 12
Xinhai Revolution 15, 69, 76-79, 81, 96
Xiong Yushan 37, 41, 48, 50, 86, 96
Xu Ruilin 38-39

Yang Hanxiang 41, 48, 56

Zhang Bishi 23
Zhao Sheng alias Zhao Boxian 50, 52-53, 121
Zhonghua Geming Dang 48-49, 122
Zhou Hua 47, 75
Zhuang Qingjian 56
Zhuang Yin'an 58-60